Living Beyond Your Losses

*The Healing Journey
Through Grief*

N. Patrick Murray, Ph.D.

MOREHOUSE PUBLISHING

Copyright © 1994 by N. Patrick Murray

Morehouse Publishing

Editorial Office:
871 Ethan Allen Hwy.
Ridgefield, CT 06877

Corporate Office:
P.O. Box 1321
Harrisburg, PA 17105

A catalog record for this book is available from the Library of Congress.

Scripture text is from the New Revised Standard Version of the Bible, copyright 1989 by the Division of Christian Education of the National Council of the Churches of Christ in the USA.

Printed in the United States of America

Table of Contents

Preface

Someone has wisely observed that "we can insult the hurt of others by giving it a meaning too quickly." This is probably one of the commonest mistakes that we make in seeking to be helpful to grieving people. I hope that no such error has been committed on the following pages.

This presentation is addressed to the grieving person who is walking through the "valley of the shadow of death," wondering if there is a way out to life again. It is drawn from many years of pastoral experience and from my own grief journey.

It is not legitimate to promise grieving persons that certain psychological techniques or spiritual secrets can be found which will magically dispel the pain of their loss. What can be minimized, however, is *needless* suffering caused by ignorance of the grief process, invalid theological precepts, or mistaken beliefs about our emotional and spiritual life. That is the motive for this essay, the basic premise of which is that to allow ourselves to grieve is to enable ourselves to grow.

—NPM

The Layers

I have walked through
many lives,
some of them my own,
and I am not who I was,
though some principle of being
abides, from which I struggle
not to stray.
When I look behind,
as I am compelled to look
before I can gather strength
to proceed on my journey,
I see the milestones dwindling
toward the horizon
and the slow fires trailing
from the abandoned camp-sites
over which scavenger angels
wheel on heavy wings.
Oh, I have made myself a tribe
out of my true affections,
and my tribe is scattered!
How shall the heart be reconciled
to its feast of losses?

In a rising wind
the manic dust of my friends,
those who fell along the way,
bitterly stings my face.
Yet I turn, I turn,
exulting somewhat,
with my will intact to go
wherever I need to go,
and every stone on the road
precious to me.

In my darkest night,
when the moon was covered
and I roamed through wreckage,
a nimbus-clouded voice
directed me:
"Live in the layers,
not on the litter."
Though I lack the art
to decipher it,
no doubt the next chapter
in my book of transformations
is already written.
I am not done with my changes.

—Stanley Kunitz[1]

Introduction

The Grief Experience

Everyday I tell myself it's time to be getting over this; I know that people expect it of me. But if anything, I'm getting worse. The first year was like a bad dream. I was clear to his bedroom door in the morning before I remembered he wasn't there to be wakened. The second year is real…. I've stopped going to his door, I've sometimes let a whole day pass by without thinking about… about him…. Now I'm far from everyone. I don't have any friends anymore, and everyone looks trivial and foolish… not related to me.

—Anne Tyler, *The Accidental Tourist*[2]

Grieving is one of the most painful, yet potentially most productive, of human experiences. This paradoxical quality invites us into the mystery and miracle of the healing journey through grief. You may be starting to read this book for one basic reason: You have suffered a loss that has thrust you into that tumultuous voyage that we call the grief process. If so, some of the following questions are likely throbbing in your mind: Will my seemingly unbearable pain ever get better? Is healing really possible after such a loss as mine? Can I hope to recover enough to find my life meaningful once again?

This presentation has one central purpose, to address these questions and offer a word of hope and affirmation. You can find life again, but you can do even more than that. Through your grief you can grow. It is true that the wound you have suffered will never entirely go away. It is now part of your life story, and as it heals the scar will remain as an indelible part of your 'character. We would not want it otherwise, because then we could not benefit from the lessons our pain has to teach us. We eventually learn that we are not so much cured *from* our grief, as *by* our grief.

In the early stages of grief, however, your pain often feels so powerful that it threatens your will to live. The abyss of sadness and despair seems to have no bottom, and sometimes you fear that you will keep sinking forever and never be able to come back. Your loss seems to have torn out the very center of your being, and you are afraid that nothing can restore you. You fear that your pain is going to overwhelm you so that you will somehow lose your ability to function as a human being. In the deep valleys of grief, it feels as if your sadness is the most powerful force in the universe. You feel that no one has ever suffered a loss as deep or painful as yours. In some respects this is true, because grieving is a highly individual process, and indeed no one has ever grieved *your* particular loss nor experienced *your* special configuration of pain.

The truth is that you are greater than your pain, and by making the healing journey you can survive it. This has been demonstrated in the lives of countless grieving persons. Marvelous recuperative powers exist within you, but your suffering may be blinding you to that realization right now. Healing forces of amazing strength are already at work, but in the initial grief period you have only limited awareness of them. Reassurances about recovery at this point certainly will not stop your grieving and may even seem offensive. However, please allow the unfolding of a roadmap that may offer a way through your present despair. Just knowing that many others before you, no wiser or better than you, have made it through this arduous journey offers a new promise of hope.

Abraham Lincoln suffered many setbacks in his life and was subject to depression. Two of his four sons died in childhood. He once said: "In this sad world of ours, sorrow comes to all, and it often comes with bitter agony. Perfect relief is not possible except with time. You cannot now believe that you will ever feel better. But this is not true. You are sure to be happy again. Knowing this, truly believing it, will make you less miserable now."[3]

In these pages you will not be offered any shortcuts or gimmicks that will prevent your having to make the grief journey, because there are none. But you will learn that you can make responses that will foster growth and healing rather than impede them. You can participate in and eventually take charge of your own recovery. No one can grieve for you, but having a map of the terrain can save a lot of needless detours and dead-ends.

What may sound like bad news at this point is that we have to pass *through* the pain, not avoid or suppress it, in order to be healed. Your grief does not have the power to destroy you, but in the recovery process it must be woven into your life story and made your friend. That does not seem like a welcome prospect right now, when grief seems to wear the face of a grotesque enemy. What we would all prefer is some means of escaping the awful hurt and returning to the life we had before our loss. This, however, is not an option. Your grief journey takes on meaning and value only as you allow it to become a pathway of emotional and spiritual growth.

This is what the spiritual traditions have long called "redemption." This classic theological term refers to the process whereby negative events and experiences are transformed into something of higher purpose and quality than originally seemed possible. The paradigm of this in the Christian tradition is the Cross and suffering of Jesus Christ on Good Friday, which eventuated in a victory over death and evil with the dawn of Easter. If we allow our suffering to take its course, we will grow, and our grief will be "redeemed" into a new quality of life that we could not have reached without undergoing it.

In some ways this redemptive growth process remains a mystery, because it interacts with the spiritual dimensions of life, which we do not fully control or understand. In other respects, however, it has some common-sense elements that are not difficult to comprehend:

1. When we suffer a severe loss we have to search out coping resources that otherwise would have lain dormant, and we are strengthened for facing life's storms. We are often told by neurologists that human beings ordinarily use only a fraction of their brain power in a life-time. Similarly, we have reservoirs of emotional and spiritual power that are not called forth until crisis confronts us.

2. After a loss, we are often required to "compensate" through new relationships and perhaps deeper friendships. We may have to widen the reach of our hearts to include others in larger ways. We may find causes worth fighting for which previously lay outside our awareness. We may establish new involvements in community, church, or civic groups, and find our eyes opened to needs that we had not seen before.

3. We are likely to be thrust into a deeper theological and spiritual quest. Doctrines such as God's providence, or the afterlife, may become less theoretical to us now and invite study, meditation, and a disciplined prayer life. We may find ourselves deeply alienated from and angry with God for allowing our loss. This may require us to re-examine our faith through spiritual direction, pastoral counseling, or growth groups.

One of the best contemporary formats for the recovery of our true spirituality has been developed by the modern twelve-step programs, which descended originally from the profound spiritual insights of the Alcoholics Anonymous movement. One thing that we have learned from these groups is that the only true and lasting recovery comes through the development of our spirituality. Finally, nothing short of this really works. This means that sooner or later we recover only through establishing a relationship with that gracious and loving Higher Power which we call God. This Power must be mediated to us through some form of healthy community, in which we establish contact with tolerant faith, realistic hope, and unconditional love.

4. We may find in our grief the invitation to enter a psychotherapeutic or counseling relationship that enlarges our

self-understanding and knits together insights about our inner emotional dynamics and the workings of our original family-system. This is essential, in fact, in cases where the grieving process becomes blocked by old wounds and unconscious forces. The grief journey involves the whole person, and will invariably reflect the emotional and spiritual state which we bring to it. Grief may break open long-standing emotional issues that are crying out to be faced and resolved. Thus, it may offer a valuable opportunity for growth through psychotherapy.

In these and many other ways, the journey of suffering is an invitation to "redemption," that is, turning something that seems only negative and destructive into a new quality of life, joy, energy, and hope. This has happened to many others who opened themselves to the healing journey, and it can happen to you. One thing is certain: the grief journey will change us. We cannot grieve and stay the same. As The Rev. Hoover Rupert, a Methodist minister, has observed, "Grief never leaves you where it finds you."

A major dimension of my own grief experience began with the birth of my third child, who was born severely challenged mentally and physically. A peculiar feature of this kind of grief experience, as all parents of developmentally disabled children know, is that it cannot come to closure.

I was reminded of this one afternoon when my older children and some of their friends ran noisily through the house, out the patio doors, into the backyard to play. My little daughter, though about five years old, was still unable to walk at that time. She crawled over to the doors and peered outside with an obvious yearning to join them. Words cannot encompass the stabbing thrust of grief that goes through a parent's heart in such a moment. Small scenes of this kind often seem to become permanently etched in our minds as a kind of microcosm of the sorrow that we can only partly express. There have been many similar scenes since that day as I have watched my daughter's struggles, defeats, and triumphs in life.

Another descent into the depths of grief began one lazy

morning in late August. As the early sunlight streamed through the curtains, I could not have believed that a day which began so bright and peaceful would end in such turmoil and pain. That morning brought my wife's sudden announcement that she wanted to end our marriage of twenty-one years.

We had no history of fighting or arguing, and there was no physical abuse nor substance-addiction in our relationship. We shared basic political and social values, and I thought we had coped quite well with the experience of parenting a severely disabled child for the previous eleven years. Somehow I had managed to rationalize the signs of her unhappiness, and therefore her words came as a total shock.

During the months that followed, I trudged through what seemed like the fathomless canyons of grief, with all its unwelcome companions of anger, anxiety, and depression. Ironically, I had long been interested in the grief process and had given lectures and workshops on the subject. This previous knowledge, however, now seemed as nothing compared to what I learned from the actual experience of grieving. Carl Jung was proven right: "One understands nothing psychologically unless one has experienced it oneself."[4]

As we begin to map the process that can lead to recovery, we must remember, however, that it is not something that works automatically, as certain natural and physical processes do. Suffering alone does not heal us; opening ourselves to the journey *through* our suffering does. Few have expressed this better than Anne Morrow Lindbergh in her book *Hour of Gold, Hour of Lead:* "I do not believe that sheer suffering teaches. If suffering alone taught, then all the world would be wise, since everyone suffers. To suffering must be added mourning, understanding, patience, love, openness and the willingness to remain vulnerable."[5]

This is the journey to which I invite you in the pages that follow. Many have walked this way before and found that it is indeed the path to new life.

Chapter One

Mapping the Grief Journey

In order to arrive there,
To arrive where you are, to get from where you are not,
You must go by a way wherein there is no ecstasy.
In order to arrive at what you do not know
You must go by a way which is the way of ignorance.
In order to possess what you do not possess
   You must go by the way of dispossession.
In order to arrive at what you are not
You must go through the way in which you are not.
And what you do not know is the only thing you know
   And what you own is what you do not own
And where you are is where you are not.

—T. S. Eliot, "East Coker," *The Four Quartets*[6]

Sooner or later, we shall all grieve. Grieving is especially associated with physical death, but actually we suffer "little deaths" in all kinds of significant losses. "If life is to be meaningful and satisfying," observes John C. Raines, "we must attach ourselves deeply and fully to people and causes. Yet everything to which we can and do attach is finite."[7] Thus, grief in some form or degree is our almost constant companion. It is vital in coping with our own and others' grieving to know something about the pattern that it generally follows. Any "mapping" of the grief journey, however, must be offered with a due amount of caution. Grief specialists have devised numerous models, postulating as many as ten "stages" in the grief process. However, all conceptual models of this kind are somewhat artificial. We do not experience the phases of the grief experience as totally discreet, and we move in and out of them cyclically as well as sequentially.

In a widely respected textbook on grief work, *The Last Dance*, Despelder and Strickland have expressed this vividly, arguing that "the actual experience resembles a series of dance steps more than it does a cross-country walk."[8] They object particulary to the use of the term "stages" in the analysis of the grief experience, warning that it can "suggest a linear progression from the first stage, through the second, and so on, until the process has been completed," whereas in fact "they are not necessarily separate; they will invariably intertwine and overlap."[9]

Any outline of the grief journey can indeed be interpreted too mechanistically, as if moving through grief is automatic, something like the stages of physical development. On the other hand, we need some kind of terminolgy to describe the passages through the grief process from its initial phase of shock and acute suffering to a place of reintegration and reestablishment.

I have found the metaphor of "mapping" the terrain of the grief journey to be useful. This flexible image suggests, for example, that there are varied and unfamiliar territories through which we must pass. It suggest that there will be twists and turns–times when we will feel lost and have to consult our "maps" and navigation intruments anew. There may be bypaths, detours, obstacles, and barriers. At times, we will likely recognize that we are still "under construction," with some distance to go before we reach the longed-for destination of recovery and greater wholeness.

As with any expedition, having a map does not prevent us from having to make the journey. However, it can be extremely valuable in delineating for us the established roadways of wisdom and experience, warning us about tempting bypaths that turn out to be dead-ends, and highlighting the signposts that previous travelers have left, reminding us that the territory has already been charted by many other pilgrims who have preceded us on this odyssey. We will explore the terrain of three realms which are well known to those who make the pilgrimage through grief: Reaction, Realization, and Recovery.

Reaction

We will use the term Reaction to describe the initial territory which we must traverse on the grief journey. This word serves to emphasize the *involuntary* character of much that happens during this acute period of impact. Primarily we experience shock. Along with shock may come a sense of disorientation, numbness, lack of memory, and the inability to make decisions or carry out normal rational thinking. In the early period of my own grief journey, I sometimes felt as if I were tumbling head over heels in a kind of "cyclotron," such as astronauts use to train for the weightlessness of outer space. These experiences can be very disconcering, but they are common and normal.

A salient feature of this initial grief period is denial of the reality of the loss. Denial mechanisms are often subtle and complex. Our defensive system is amazingly "creative" during this period in helping us rationalize. We may pass through layer after layer of denial, often grasping at straws to fabricate illusions that the loss will somehow go away. Such is the power of the denial mechanism. However, it serves a vital function of protecting us from the full immediate impact of our loss and allows valuable time for our coping resources to be amassed.

The Reaction period thus seems to activate some natural protective mechanisms when we need them most, so that we can survive the initial shock. They enable us to go through the motions that are required: a funeral, packing and loading for a move, or working out a divorce settlement, for example. We often look back, however, with the feeling that we partly did these things in a kind of zombie-like state, not yet really feeling the pain of the loss. All of this is normal and probably merciful in the early phase of the grief process.

The Reaction period can last from a few hours to a few weeks, but certainly longer in severe losses. If you fear that you are stranded in this initial phase, it is imperative to obtain specialized help from support systems and therapists in order to move on. Some signs of being stuck are (1) inability to talk about the loss, (2) failure to resume normal social patterns (attending church, clubs, hobbies), (3) obsessive/compulsive behavior and emotional rigidity, (4) inability to face required tasks (straighten out financial matters, deal appropriately with property and possessions, for example), and (5) talking and acting as if the loss has not really happened or is not permanent.

Give yourself the gift of calling upon understanding friends, pastors, physicians, and other helpers for the support you need. Ultimately, it is true that we have to do our grief work alone, but we do not have to *be* alone. Opening yourself to a community of caring people, even though you may feel like remaining isolated, may prove to be the single most important element in your recovery.

Furthermore, it may be necessary in the early critical days of grief, to rely upon an appropriate medication from the many now available for severe stress and trauma. In pastoral work, it is common to encounter resistance and guilt over the use of pharmaceutical remedies for what are considered to be emotional and spiritual problems. People fear that reliance on medication will artificially numb their faculties and retard the real healing process. This is a worthy instinct and may indeed be appropriate at a later stage.

No one wants to lower unduly the threshold of caution in view of the current epidemic of drug abuse. Nonetheless, the excessive fear of medication often betrays a belief in a false dichotomy between the physical and spiritual realm. Our nature is essentially holistic and ultimately belies this split. It is needlessly cruel to deny oneself the relief of God-given medications, which can often restore us to a level of functioning that enables our "higher" spiritual and rational faculties to mobilize more effectively for recovery. Of course one must choose a competent medical practitioner who understands holistic medicine and will monitor carefully any tendencies toward addiction, regulating dosages accordingly.

In extreme loss such as death or divorce, the first year may be spent mostly in Reaction, just getting one's head above water and overcoming the terrible sense of disorientation common to this initial period. Completing that first year is a major accomplishment, for we must carry our loss for the first time through the whole cycle of anniversaries, birthdays, holidays, and special family observances. Thus, in major loss a year may be required for working through shock and denial and for gaining strength to move on and face one's deeper pain.

Realization

The second phase of the grief process we could term Realization. As the natural buffering mechanisms of the Reaction stage begin to dissolve, the implications of the loss increasingly permeate our awareness and feelings flood in. The emotions most common to this middle stage are guilt, anger, anxiety, and depression. Physical symptoms may appear also, in the form of headaches, sleep disturbances, reduced immunities, gastro-intestinal disorders, and frequent sighing.

Unfortunately, it is possible for grief wounds to become "infected," in Howard Clinebell's insightful term, and fail to heal properly. This can leave one stalled in the grief process, unable to move on toward Recovery. Sandra was a young woman in her mid-thirties, the oldest of several children, who came to see me about a current problem in her life.[10] It soon became apparent, however, that a past trauma was seriously affecting her present adjustment to life. About 23 years before, when Sandra was 13, her three-year old sister whom she adored had been run over and killed by a truck.

Sandra went through several forms of denial, including

the hope that God would miraculously bring her little sister back to life. Her family was never able to grieve through this tragic event. Their way was to close ranks and go on as if it had not happened. Family members never shared their feelings about their loss. As commonly happens, Sandra's childhood mind interpreted this to mean that it was all too terrible to face, so she gradually repressed her grief feelings. In doing so, she essentially remained in the Reaction phase for well over twenty years.

Through many months of diligent therapeutic work, Sandra was able to unearth her long-standing pain and work through her grief for her little sister. One day she reported the following dream:

> *I and several family members go to the cemetery where my sister and others in the family are buried. However, it is not a forlorn place, but has a park-like atmosphere, with many people around. We arrive in a big old green convertible and unpack lots of suitcases, coolers and picnic supplies. I leave for a while and go driving around alone. When I return, they are packing and preparing to leave. I decide to put the top up on the convertible but get tangled up in it. I manage to get loose. As we load the car, I notice a small, brown, beat-up looking suitcase that hasn't been loaded. It belongs to us, but my uncle keeps saying there isn't room for it and that it should stay. My great aunt is indecisive and is afraid of doing the wrong thing. My mother says, "Well, whatever you think." Very reluctantly, I go along with leaving it behind. As we leave, I look back one last time at the suitcase. It looks very small and very much alone as we drive away.*

Sandra and I gradually came to see that the dream was predictive. It previewed an approaching resolution of her long-standing grief process, as she finally resolved to leave the little suitcase behind at the cemetery. The burial place is not dreadful or despairing, but has a park-like atmosphere where people can be happy (having picnics). The dream indicated significant individuation on Sandra's part, as she left the crowd and went driving alone.

Within a few months, she did indeed move on through the deep sorrow she had carried so long and became a more near-ly whole and happy person. Though the process often cost her a great deal of pain, she achieved remarkable emotional and spiritual growth. Sandra's words were: "It feels like I've come to a resting-place—at least for a time. I feel good about the work I've done. I feel good about who I've become and I am curious about what lies ahead."

Guilt is among the most common emotions marking the Realization period, and it also has the potential to become infected. It is evidenced by statements like, "If only I had tried other doctors, treatments, clinics..." "If only I had tried hard-er to make the relationship work." "If only I had been kinder." "It was my idea to do... If we hadn't, maybe it wouldn't have happened." We can best help ourselves and others here by our allowing such feelings to register in consciousness, but then gently confronting them with a more reasonable perspective.

Some years ago, a middle-aged industrial engineer was referred to me by a physician because his malaise seemed to extend well beyond his medical problems. He was in fact depressed to the point of feeling suicidal. "Sometimes when I am flying," he said, "I think about how I wouldn't care if the plane went down. It would get me out of my misery." On a family vacation about two years earlier his teen-age son had drowned in a swimming accident. This man was carrying an enormous load of unresolved guilt, typical of grieving persons, who often blame themselves for their loss. "It was my idea to take the vacation," he said. "If only we had gone a different route or not stopped at that motel, my son would not have died."

Such ideas are manifestly irrational, of course, to the objective listener. The "if onlys" that our minds can conjure when we are under a load of guilt seem almost limitless. Part of the mystery of why this kind of irrational guilt can be so per-sistent may lie in "survivor's guilt," as discussed/named by Eric

Lindemann in his pioneering studies. The father's grief was compounded by the sense of unfairness over his young son's being deprived of life when he, who had lived much longer, still survived. With this kind of "infected" guilt, we need experienced helping persons to reflect firmly the unreality and unreasonableness of the ideas fueling the guilt, while, at the same time, providing all possible support for working through the pain of the loss.

I suspect that another reason for irrational self-blame in grief is that it provides a defense against an even more painful emotion: the fear that life's events are random and our tragedies utterly meaningless. Severe loss can shatter philosophical and theological anchors on which we have traditionally relied. Blaming oneself, painful as it is, at least offers some "explanation" for why terrible things happen: we can attribute them to our own ineptitude or failure. (See the discussion of self-forgiveness in Chapter Two, "The Cost of Forgiveness.")

Anger also is very likely to surface during the Realization Stage. It may be directed toward the medical community or other helping professions. This is exacerbated in a society that holds a quasi-magical view of modern medical science. Curiously, anger may be directed even at the one who has died, even though the rational mind knows that the person could not help dying. God is also a common target of anger in our grief. This is especially likely to be evoked in persons who believe that God directly wills and causes every event in the world. Unfortunately, this form of anger often gets repressed because of social teaching that it is unacceptable or even blasphemous.

In a grief experience the cry of the heart often becomes, "Why did God let this happen?" Through many years of pastoral work, I have come to regard this as the single most troubling issue raised by grieving people. It lands us squarely in the center of what theology long ago labeled the "problem of evil," which has never been satisfactorily resolved. It seems ironic that one of theology's most intractable issues can be articulated in such simple terms: "If God is so powerful and loving, why does he allow innocent suffering?" For persons in grief this is no mere intellectual conundrum, but becomes an urgent issue of spiritual survival. (We will examine this in greater detail in Chapter Five, "Something There Is That Power Destroys.")

A misguided piece of popular piety is fond of telling grieving people that they are not supposed to ask the "Why me?" questions. Presumably a more noble approach is to look around us at all the sorrow in the world and stoically decide that we have no more reason to be exempt from suffering than anyone else. Some add an even stronger reproach and admonish us to ask instead, "Why *not* me?" All of this is an absurd piece of piosity bordering on cruelty.

When struck by a severe loss, persons with a faith orientation will instinctively ask the "Why me?" question. Not to allow them to raise this issue is to risk engendering needless guilt and even the collapse of their theological foundations. Without being able to express honestly our anger and hurt toward God, we are likely to experience a deepening alienation from our spiritual resources just when we need them most.

Another strong emotion that accompanies grief is the feeling that others' lives all around us are proceeding in a normal, happy way, while our lives are in shambles. We see jolly families on their back-yard patios; we observe smiling couples in restaurants; we see folks celebrating wedding anniversaries; we get Christmas letters recounting family successes of the past year; and we ask, "Why are other lives so full of happiness while mine is so shattered?" It is not that we resent the good fortune of others or wish it otherwise. Rather, we are tortured by questions like "Why is it different for me? Could this be a punishment for something I have done? Do others know some secret of living that I have never gotten in on?"

These sentiments are not realistic, but they are almost invariable accompaniments of the grief experience, especially in its early stages. They are *feelings*, not rational deductions, and must be treated as such. Feelings do not ask if they can happen. They are simply what they are. They are neither moral nor immoral. Feelings do not play on the field of moral judgment, whereas behaviors do. *Feeling* hungry, for example, is not a moral issue; stealing to satisfy hunger is. *Feeling* anger is neither morally right nor wrong; acting out anger so as to injure someone involves us immediately in legal and moral questions. *Having* sexual feelings is not a moral question; how we act upon them, however, involves complex moral judgments.

When, as grief-stricken people, we *feel* that God or "life" has singled us out for special suffering, we need a safe support community which will allow us to have these feelings. We will not be helped by attempts to argue us out of our feelings, or, far worse, by being told that our feelings are morally and spiritually deficient. What we are expressing is simply a fundamental symptom of the grief experience. Painful attitudes and feelings that do not match with reality can only be healed by letting them come forth into conscious awareness and having them accepted. Then they are much less likely to be acted out in some unhealthy way.

It is crucial for helping people to understand that *accepting* people's feelings is entirely different from *agreeing* with them When we are made to feel guilty about feelings, we usuall banish them to the "basement" of our minds, where they fester and may eventually manifest themselves in disguise through various psychosomatic and anxiety disorders. (See more on dealing with anger in Chapter Two, "The Cost of Forgiveness.")

One of the most difficult aspects of the Realization period is the experience of waiting. Waiting is the dreadful season of "in between." We have moved past the experience of the original trauma, which at least contained drama and intensity. During that time we likely received attention and support from others. Then the weary days wore on and they resumed their normal routine; we did not. They gradually forgot about our loss and sadness; our memories remained vivid.

During Realization we have lost the protective features of the Reaction period, but we have not yet reached a place of resolution of our pain. We know Recovery only as the promise of a distant realm, and we are not sure if we shall reach it. We

do not know if we can live again, or love again, or risk ourselves in a close relationship again. We do not know if the pain
will ever stop throbbing, for when it seems to abate, it later
returns with renewed fury. We are not yet free of the "demon"
of our sorrow, and we are not sure if any power can exorcize it.

In the Christian liturgical calendar, with its dramatic
march through salvation history, much is made of the dark
tragedy of Good Friday and of the wonder and mystery of
Easter. But the day between, Holy Saturday, receives no special attention. Perhaps this day should be reclaimed and dedi-
cated to the grieving. Holy Saturday symbolizes the time of
waiting, the awful season of in-between, when the initial
drama and passion of our loss has faded, but we are yet a long
way from the time of healing.

Try to imagine the despair of the little band of forlorn disciples on that first Holy Saturday. Their high hopes for this
Jesus of Nazareth lay shattered. Gone was the heady excite-
ment of those early days when they thought the long-awaited
Messiah had finally come. Now they huddled in the back
streets of Jerusalem, afraid for their lives, in case Jesus' death
should unleash a backlash against those who had associated
with him. The quiet misery of Holy Saturday was different
from the horror of Good Friday, which at least had its frenzy
and distraction. Now the pain was only a dull ache, but it had
the feel of permanence and seemed to reach to the bone. All
grieving persons know about the Holy Saturday experience.
They know that the season of waiting is often a time when our
support-system is at a minimum and our pain is at a maximum.

In Samuel Beckett's play *Waiting for Godot* two hapless
characters, Estragon and Vladimir, wait by a crossroad for a
mysterious figure who is supposed to be arriving soon. They
anticipate that his coming somehow will solve their problems
and infuse meaning into their lives. Very soon, however, we
sense that we are witnessing a cycle of utter futility. They are
waiting for a fantasy. Nothing at all is going to happen. Becket
achieves an uncanny and all-engulfing sense of absolute *stasis*.
Any illusion of forward motion in the drama fades away, and

we know we are trapped in pathetic and endless repetition.

A play of this magnitude and brilliance can, of course, be variously interpreted. I take it to be a commentary on the character of modern culture, much of which has lost contact with the traditional Hebrew-Christian metaphor of life as a journey. The name Godot may be seen as a variant of the word "God." The promise of God's coming is regarded as illusory, and thus the play seems reflective of the profound despair in contemporary life. Lost is the expectation of a Healing Power that meets us in suffering with the grace of new life. Waiting becomes meaningless.

The motif of "waiting upon the Lord," on the other hand, runs throughout the Biblical story. Waiting is the pathway to healing, but Biblical waiting is always active and expectant, not passive. One of the Old Testament prophets, Habakkuk, probably wrote about 600 B.C. when the Jewish people were under the tyrannical heel of Babylon. It was a time of profound grieving. He stood upon a watchtower and challenged God with these words: "O Lord, how long shall I cry for help and thou wilt not hear? Or cry to thee 'Violence!' and thou will not save? Why dost thou make me see wrongs and look upon trouble?" (1:2-3)

The answer that God sends is not always easy for grieving people to receive. God assures Habakkuk that he is already at work bringing redemption but that this healing work is hidden from the prophet's eyes at present. Then God says, "For still the vision awaits its time—it will not lie. If it seem slow, wait for it." (2:3) God's answer to Habakkuk may sound understated. In the pain of grief the "vision" *always* seems slow. Waiting for some way to envision how God's hand is working in our lives may be the most challenging element of faith during the anguish of the Realization period.

We hear the theme of waiting throughout the psalms. The author of the 40th psalm voices it beautifully: "I waited patiently upon the Lord. He stooped to me and heard my cry. He lifted me out of the desolate pit, out of the mire and clay; he set my feet upon a high cliff and made my footing sure. He put a new song in my mouth, a song of praise to our God."

Job waited for God's voice through his terrible ordeals, crying, "Though he slay me, yet will I trust him" (13:15, King James Version). Isaiah experienced the grace that comes through waiting, describing it with characteristic eloquence: "Those who wait upon the Lord shall renew their strength, they shall mount up with wings like eagles, they shall run and not be weary, they shall walk and not faint." (40:31 NRSV)

Because every grief journey is unique, once again it is arbitrary to place a time-frame on the Realization period. It may involve as much as two years in severe losses like death or divorce, and sometimes even longer. Isaiah, Habakkuk, and the author of psalm 40 do not tell us how *long* they "waited upon the Lord." The healing process, moreover, is never one of smooth and steady movement like the graceful ascent of a jetliner. Rather, progress comes in fits and starts. The climb out of grief is more like a sawtooth pattern, with "up" periods of affirmation intermixed with "down" times of despair.

Even after that first difficult year, low times may be precipitated by anniversaries of the loss, as well as birthdays, holidays, and other significant points in family history. In down times, we often feel that all our hard-won progress has been lost and that the struggle is for naught. In time, however, we come to see that the sawtooth motion has been gradually upward. This is not an uncommon experience in the life of faith generally. The hand of providence often seems more clearly discernible in retrospect than in the present moment. Soren Kierkegaard said, "Life can only be understood backwards; but it must be lived forwards."

In some ways, Realization is the most difficult of the three phases of grief. It is possible to get stuck here and wander indefinitely in a welter of regrets and sorrows. As we have emphasized, the ministry of a wise and nurturing support community is probably a person's most valuable resource during this critical period. At few other times is it more emphatically true that "it is not good for man to be alone." (Genesis 2:18)

Recovery

No distinct line marks the passage from Realization to the final period of grief, Recovery, the season of healing. It is something like our movement into "maturity," where no single threshold is passed. Lynn Caine in her book *Widow* has given an eloquent summary of the Recovery experience: "...bereavement is a wound. It's like being very, very badly hurt... You will grieve and that is painful. And your grief will have many stages, but all of them will be healing. Little by little, you will be whole again. And you will be a stronger person. Just as a broken bone knits and becomes stronger than before, so will you."[11]

Important signs of recovery are rejoining society, returning to responsibility and ministry, searching out new ways to live creatively, and developing means of "compensation" for the loss. In short, recovery is marked by the balanced and sober incorporation of reality without the need for denial, escape, or undue blame of self and others. We gradually discover once again that "the light shines on in the darkness, and the darkness has not put it out." (John 1:5)

A word of caution is necessary, however, about what is meant by "recovery." A grief-experience is woven into our spiritual and emotional character and leaves a permanent legacy of change. A healthy recovery does not require us to "accept" our loss in the sense of a return to life as it was before. This is impossible, and expecting it from ourselves could become a source of needless guilt. The post-resurrection narratives, particularly in the Fourth Gospel, recount that Jesus carried the scars of the Cross into eternity. Redemption does not mean the *cancellation* of our life story, but rather having it taken up into a higher order of meaning. The Very Reverend Alan Jones, Dean of Grace Cathedral in San Francisco, wisely observes: "...the really creative and free souls I have encountered all have been shipwrecked at one time or another. They have had their world taken from them and lived to tell the tale."[12]

A rabbinic tale beautifully illustrating this tells of an ancient Jewish community which faithfully followed the practice of rending their garments as an expression of grief. One day, some of the faithful approached their rabbis with the practical question as to whether garments which had been thus torn could be sewn up and used again after the prescribed period of mourning. The rabbis sensed the implications of the question and took it under advisement. Finally, they returned with the decision that such garments could indeed be mended, but the seams must never be tucked in so as to make it appear that the garments had never been torn.

The wise rabbis understood a fundamental truth about the grief experience. Although healing comes, the marks of our wounding are permanent. Thus, as grief counselor Dennis Klass has said, we are not called upon to "get over" our grief in one sense, for "this would mean we were not changed by the experience. It would mean we did not grow by the experience."

Some years ago a seminary dean suffered the tragic loss of his son. After a time away for grieving, he returned to the seminary community and gave a chapel address in which he said, "I have been to the bottom, and I want to report to you that it is solid." That is an incisive statement of what it means to recover from grief. In the Recovery phase we learn that what we thought was a fathomless abyss of sorrow and futility has a limit after all. Healing resources are available to help us climb out again, where the sunlight reappears.

People discover as they move into Recovery that they can actually learn to give thanks for their grief. Do not dismiss this idea prematurely as bizarre or insensitive. During particularly painful periods, it is helpful to meditate on the thought, "I am grateful for being able to feel my pain." This will bring into awareness the most encouraging truth about all grief: namely, that in opening ourselves to it we can grow emotionally and spiritually. It is not easy to reach the realm of the grateful heart, but it is one of the rewards of making the healing journey. It is a very significant mark of spiritual growth. For most of us it is a long journey through which God has to lead us. It does not happen overnight.

A grateful heart means that we have begun to accept the

pain and brokenness of our lives and to become reconciled to it. It means that we have learned how to grieve through our broken dreams, our dashed hopes, and yet find God's strength sufficient. Every grateful heart was first of all a broken heart. Jesus said, "Blessed are the poor in spirit (broken in spirit), for theirs is the kingdom of heaven." It is indeed true that only grateful hearts can truly enter the kingdom, for grateful hearts have faced their brokenness and accepted healing from a Power greater than themselves. That is what it means to enter the Kingdom of God.

George Herbert's great old prayer says, "Thou that hast given so much to me, Give one thing more, a grateful heart." Of all the things we can pray for, why should we ask for such an odd gift as "a grateful heart"? Some words of the Benedictine monk, David Steindl-Rast, help to answer this question:

> *Thanksgiving, where it is genuine, does not primarily look at the gift and express appreciation; it looks at the giver and expresses trust. The courageous confidence that trusts in the Giver of all gifts is faith. To give thanks even when we cannot see the goodness of the Giver, to learn this is to find the path to peace of heart. For happiness is not what makes us grateful. It is gratefulness that makes us happy.*[13]

The grateful heart gains understanding of one of life's most basic lessons: joy does not come from the absence of suffering, but from the presence of God.

A grateful heart also will help to place us in gentle and loving touch with our Inner Self, reminding us that our capacity to feel and to grieve is at the same time our capacity to love. We are in grief because we loved something deeply, and loving is the richest and most profound human experience. It is what makes us human beings. Cutting the nerve of our grief admittedly would stop the pain, but it would render us nothing more than unfeeling robots without the richness of our humanity. Therefore, how can anyone truly wish to be unable to grieve?

Grief is always an invitation to undergo the death of the old

self and discover a new relationship with our true self. This
experience has been traditionally described as spiritual "rebirth." It is the birth of renewed hope for us who feel desperate
and forlorn, the birth of courage for us who feel afraid of the
future or wear the cloak of sadness, the birth of creativity and
energy in us who feel weary and worn out with the burdens of
life. One of the classic stories about this birth of the inner self
is told in St. John's Gospel, and tells of an encounter between
Jesus and a man named Nicodemus:

> *Now there was a Pharisee named Nicodemus, a leader of the
> Jews. He came to Jesus by night and said to him, "Rabbi, we
> know that you are a teacher who has come from God; for no
> one can do these signs that you do apart from the presence of
> God." Jesus answered him, "Very truly, I tell you, no one
> can see the kingodom of God without being born from
> above." Nicodemus said to him, "How can any one be born
> after having grown old? Can one enter a second time into
> the mother's womb and be born?" (John 3:1-4, NRSV)*

Nicodemus no doubt came to Jesus for a reason that is both
simple and complex—he knew that something was missing in
his life. He didn't have a name for it; he couldn't really diag-
nose it; he just knew that he needed something that he didn't
have. It is in just such moments, paradoxically, that the potential for new life arises within us.

Let us enter this story through the awareness that our
name also is Nicodemus, and he is our spokesman. Our questions are the same as his: What is this promise of new life, this
hope that something can fill the awful void created by our
grief? Jesus sensed Nicodemus' need that night and said to
him, "Unless a person is born anew, from above, he cannot
see the Kingdom, the Higher Power in his life." And then
Nicodemus voices one of the profoundest issues of Recovery
as he asks: "But how can someone be born anew when he is
old?"

Like Nicodemus, *we* are also "old." We are old in our brokenness; we are old in our childhood fears; we are old in our stale bondage to compulsive or addictive behaviors that rob us of joy; we are old from our hurts, and griefs, and losses. We are old in our loneliness and fear of an uncertain future; we are old in our mistakes and failures; we are old from our broken hopes and dreams that will never come true. And how can we be born anew when we are old? Unless there is an answer to that question, then Recovery will seem always beyond our reach.

The new birth that must take place is the birth of the child within you. The true child, or true self, within us is that center from which we draw our creativity, our spontaneity, our energy, our depth of feeling, our wellspring of life, and our joy. Carl Jung called it the "Divine Child" within. I believe it is what the Bible means by "the image of God" in each human being. It is the inexpressibly beautiful human self as it came fresh from God's hand at our birth. Sadly, the Divine Child in many of us has been stifled, rejected, abused, and made guilty and ashamed by lack of nurture and love.

As grieving persons seeking recovery, we likewise ask Nicodemus' question: "How can we be born anew when we are old?" Jesus gave an answer, and it is for us too. The new birth, he said, has to happen through a Power greater than us, to which we learn to open ourselves. We finally experience this more as a gift than an achievement, something which we cannot manipulate or control. This is what the religious traditions mean by the word "grace." Because the grief experience drives us to the limits of our strength and threatens to exhaust our familiar coping resources, it puts us in a position to experience grace.

All grieving is a kind of death experience, as we are forced to let go of something that has given us "life." In this place of extreme spiritual and emotional vulnerability, we often find ourselves broken open to a healing power that we had not known about before. We invite this power into our lives with words like those of Jesus at the hour of his death: "Into your hands, I commend my spirit."

Shortly before his death in 1961, Dag Hammarskjöld, the second Secretary-General of the United Nations, spoke of this act of self-surrender to our Higher Power:

I don't know Who—or what—put the question. I don't know when it was put. I don't even remember answering. But at some moment I did answer Yes to Someone—or Something—and from that hour I was certain that existence is meaningful and that, therefore, my life, in self-surrender, had a goal.[14]

It comes when we give up control, and open ourselves to receive the gift. This, however, is never accomplished in only one moment of decision, but will require us to descend through layer after layer of pain and denial before we are fully open to the miracle of grace.

The grief journey often discloses to us that long ago we learned to reject the Divine Child within us. Perhaps we were taught that he or she was not good enough, or pretty enough, or capable enough, or something enough. And so that beautiful child within, with all its creative energy and capacity for joy, has been partially lost to us, hiding behind walls of early childhood defenses. But it is not dead, and ironically when we grieve we are placed in touch with our inner child in fresh ways that open up the possibility of healing growth.

That is what Nicodemus was seeking that night, and what we are longing for too. It is the miracle of new life, even when we are "old." We may not know how we can enter the womb of life again and be born. But the Power behind all life knows, and that is why the new birth continues to happen where people are willing to ask again in sincerity, "Show me how to be born anew even though I am 'old'."

Dealing with our grief opens us to this experience of rebirth. As John Bradshaw has said, "We have to learn to face our pain and feel it and get through it. One of the first steps is to recognize our lost-child self and grieve for the pain. We have to learn to grieve—for ourselves, for our families, for our wasted lives. Because grieving completes the past. And the end of grieving is to be reborn."[15]

The journey to recovery may also be described as an experience of "resurrection," the birth of the true self. In one of his poems Carl Sandburg asks a probing question about the birth of Jesus at Christmas, but it applies to the birth of the Divine Child in every person at any time:

> *Shall all wanderers over the earth, all homeless ones,*
> *All against whom doors are shut and words spoken—*
> *Shall these find the earth less strange tonight?*
> *Shall they hear news, a whisper on the night wind?*
> *"A child is born."*

When we open ourselves to our inner child, listening for the whisper of the Spirit on the night wind, the answer is forever "Yes!"

Chapter Two

The Cost of
Forgiveness

In sorrow we begin slowly to let the anger and the self-pity go. We begin to think that we can know happiness again—not an innocent happiness, but an adult and seasoned happiness. It is a happiness with shadows, but it has found a way to affirm those shadows.

—John C. Raines[16]

Forgiveness breaks the chain of causality because he who "forgives" you—out of love—takes upon himself the consequences of what you have done. Forgiveness, therefore, always entails a sacrifice. The price you must pay for your own liberation through another's sacrifice is that you in turn must be willing to liberate in the same way, irrespective of the consequences to yourself.

—Dag Hammarskjöld[17]

Grief is often caused by rejection or hurt that we suffer at the hands of others, which presents the grieving person with the issue of forgiveness. One of the most common admonitions offered to persons who have suffered abuse or injustice is "You must forgive," but popular concepts of forgiveness often harbor some serious misapprehensions. It is often understood as a simple act of will, to be achieved in a one-time decision. This, however, would be like trying to eat one huge meal that would last a lifetime. Forgiveness is far more complex than that, and like the whole grief process, requires a journey through several layers of the heart.

Despite its unfortunate title, one of the best recent manuals on the subject of forgiveness has been written by Lewis B. Smedes. His book, *Forgive and Forget*, offers a helpful outline of four stages of the forgiving process:

(1) We acknowledge the hurt, facing whatever has happened and allowing it to come fully into conscious awareness.

(2) We own our feelings of hatred, blame, and anger. Denial or repression of these inevitable emotions stalls the engine of forgiveness.

(3) We accept the need to heal ourselves. In this step we take responsibility for our own life and spiritual growth, severing the need to blame and get even.

(4) We wish the other person well and offer the opportunity for a restored relationship. Of course the kind of relationship that is possible partly depends on the other person, but we open the door from our side.[18]

Another common misapprehension of forgiveness is reminiscent of Dietrich Bonhoeffer's warnings about "cheap grace." It might be termed "cheap forgiveness," in which one piously tries to say something like, "What you did was okay." It is reflected in the cliché, "forgive and forget." But forgiveness and forgetting are not at all the same thing. It would be disastrous to our spirituality if we did not remember our own story and all that has happened on our journey. Forgiveness is not just ignoring the injustice that has been suffered, but rather is the choice not to retaliate. It does not merely say "It's okay," which would discount the relationship as unimportant, but says "I wish for you continued growth and insight, and do not choose to get even."

In the mid 1980s, The Reverend Lawrence Jenco, a Roman Catholic priest, was held hostage in Lebanon for 594 days by a radical Islamic group. He was in solitary confinement for about six months. After his release he stated that he did not hold animosity toward his often-brutal captors. In a book he later wrote about his ordeal he said, however: "I don't believe that forgetting is one of the signs of forgiveness. I forgive, but I remember. I do not forget the pain, the loneliness, the ache, the terrible injustice. But I do not remember to inflict some future retribution."[19]

Forgiveness continues to lift the offender to the Healing Power, interceding for the person's fullest possible well-being. Perhaps the most succinct summary of genuine forgiveness is found in Jesus' words: "Love your enemies, do good to those who hate you, bless those who curse you, pray for those who abuse you." (Luke 6:27 NRSV)

Learning to handle our anger is another crucial aspect of the forgiving process. A healthy spirituality understands that anger is not the enemy of forgiveness. Genuine forgiveness, in fact, can occur only in those who have fully experienced their anger and established the boundaries of the self. John Bradshaw has given us a most perceptive insight about anger when he calls it the "emotion of dignity."[20] The Latin root of the word "dignity" means "worth." In experiencing our anger over abuse and injustice, we assert our innate worth. We are saying, "I have personal boundaries that are not to be violated." This affirms that our selfhood is a holy thing.

It seems obvious, therefore, that any attempt at "forgiveness" prior to the appropriation of our anger is doomed to be unauthentic. Until we have embraced our own dignity, our attempts at forgiveness will reflect passivity and weakness. Forgiveness is the transcendence of anger, not the denial or repression of it. In forgiveness we discover that, despite the injustice we have suffered, our anger does not have to control our behavior. We assume the stance of wishing what is best for the one who has transgressed our boundaries, refusing to trade in kind, not returning hurt for hurt. (See Matthew 5:38-39)

An important question arises at this point: what is the difference between anger and hatred? Much confusion surrounds this issue, and the consequences are often emotionally damaging. Anger is a *feeling*; hatred is an *attitude*. As we have previously emphasized, feelings do not "play on the field" of morality. They are not willed, and therefore are not legitimate subjects for moral injunctions such as, "You should not feel that way," or "You ought not to be angry." We do not choose to have emotions; they simply *are*. They arise from deep within our fundamental physiological and psychological make-up, and in many respects are essential to our survival. Hunger feelings, for example, remind us to nourish the body. Sexual feelings help to insure the perpetuation of the human race. Anger is a warning signal that our well-being, at least as we perceive it, is in some kind of danger. It is our choices about the *expression* of emotions that belong in the realm of moral evaluation, not feelings themselves. Feeling hungry is morally neutral; stealing to satisfy hunger is not. Behavior involves morality; feelings do not.

Hatred, on the other hand, is attitudinal. Attitudes, unlike feelings, do indeed come within the range of our will, once we become aware of them. Hence, they are legitimate subjects of moral education. Prejudice, for example, is an attitude. It is based on distorted perceptions or faulty moral education. While we may not directly choose our prejudices at first, we certainly can decide to change them under the influence of effective moral and spiritual guidance.

Love is complicated by the fact that it is both a feeling and an attitude. It would be a great help if English, like Greek, provided separate words for the complex levels and facets of what we label generically as "love." The Christian understanding of love, as expressed in the Greek *agape*, is clearly attitudinal, and the New Testament contains numerous injunctions to incorporate this attitude into our moral and spiritual character. (See, for example, St. Paul's hymn to *agape* in I Corinthians 13.)

This should be obvious in Jesus' commandment that we are to love our enemies and indeed pray for those who hurt and abuse us. (Matthew 5:43-45) If we interpret the word "love" here merely as a feeling, this injunction is contradictory and absurd. By definition, enemies are those whom we do *not* love (have good feelings toward)!

Love as a *feeling* is just like the other examples of feelings that we have discussed. It is not directly willed, and therefore cannot provide an adequate foundation on which to base moral behavior. Moral judgment requires us to evaluate feelings before we act upon them.[21]

This discussion enables us to see that anger is not the opposite of love. In fact, the two cannot be separated. Only when our selfhood has the strength of its anger do we have the capacity truly to love. We cannot envision anyone with strong character lacking the ability to be angry! Jesus was often angry. On at least one occasion he was furious with Simon Peter. (See Matthew 16:23, and the discussion of Jesus' temptations in Chapter Five below.) He was probably angry with Judas on the night of his betrayal as he told him to "Go and do quickly" what he had plotted. He frequently expressed vehement anger at the Scribes and Pharisees, and he drove the money changers out of the temple with a whip. However, it is inconceivable to attribute hatred to Jesus, or to anyone with highly developed moral and spiritual character. Jesus prayed even for his executioners in a time of supreme agony on the Cross.

Forgiveness, therefore, does not necessitate giving up our anger, but it does require that we overcome the attitude of hatred. Since we do not will our feelings of anger in the first place, we cannot simply decide to forego them. However, we sometimes repress them. Repressing anger sacrifices our selfhood, and destroys our ability to protect the innate worth of ourselves and others.

Hatred, on the other hand, is the *attitude* of wishing ill or harm upon others. It is a debased and primitive response, which lies at the root of most of the suffering, injustice, and violence in human history. Hatred does not serve the cause of justice. In fact, when moral and legal judgments are made out of hatred, they are almost certain to be unjust! Hatred, not anger, is the opposite of forgiveness.

We can imagine only one class of people who could live without needing to forgive, and that would be persons who had reached spiritual and moral perfection. Presumably, they would never experience hurt in the first place, because in their completeness they would always understand why people do things and what the extenuating circumstances were. The question of forgiving would never arise for them, because forgiveness, at least in its fullest sense, only comes into play when we cannot understand why others have hurt us.

Another reason why perfect people would never need to practice forgiveness is that they would never need it themselves. A conversation allegedly took place once between John Wesley and General Oglethorpe. The general was heard to say to Wesley, "I never forgive!" And Wesley said in reply, "Then I hope, sir, you never sin."[22] Perfect people could rest assured that they would never make mistakes or act out of their blindness and brokenness. The rest of us, however, are forever bound up with the brokenness of the whole human family. We are denied the luxury of being unforgiving, if we intend to ask for that same kind of compassion from others.

Forgiveness learns to say, "I believe that the part of you that has caused hurt is not the whole 'you'. I want that true self to come alive, even though you have hurt me, and I still believe that it can. Someone has done painful things to you, or you would never have learned how to do painful things to others." This was what Jesus understood when he prayed even for his executioners: "Father, forgive them, for they know not what they do."

We cannot limit our giving of this healing love to others, or it will stop flowing to *us*. If we stop the outflow of water from a channel, the inflow will cease too. Only perfect people can afford to stop that flow. This is the meaning of the petition in the Lord's Prayer which says, "Forgive us our trespasses, as we forgive those who trespass against us." This same spiritual principle is voiced in the Beatitude which says, "Blessed are the merciful, for they shall obtain mercy."

Jesus once said to Simon Peter, "No, you don't just forgive seven times; you forgive seventy times seven." (Matthew 18:21-22) Jesus understood that forgiveness is not contingent upon the repentance or remorse of the offender. Sometimes those who hurt us later realize what they have done and express regret, but more often they do not. Our forgiveness of others cannot await this uncertain outcome and actually has nothing to do with it. If we wait for others to be sorry that they have injured us, we will usually wait forever. The forgiving spirit is a quality within the forgiver, and is not dependent upon the moral caliber of the offender. Our spiritual growth must proceed regardless of what others do. The three "Cs" of recovery programs remind us that we did not *cause* them to be like they are; we cannot *control* it; and we won't be able to *cure* it.

Legend has it that when Leonardo Da Vinci was painting "The Last Supper," he decided to paint the likeness of Judas Iscariot as the face of one of his enemies. It was a clever way to have some revenge on someone he hated. So, gloatingly, he painted his enemy's face onto Judas Iscariot. However, as he tried to complete the painting, he could never get a vision of how he wanted to paint the face of Jesus. Time dragged by as Leonardo searched for the appropriate face to paint for Jesus. All the while, Leonardo was bothered by the fact that he had painted his enemy as Judas. Finally, he painted out the face of the man that he hated, and replaced it with a neutral likeness for Judas. That night, in a dream he saw the face of Jesus just as he knew it had to be painted, and he quickly completed his masterpiece.

Likewise, the unforgiving spirit toward those who have hurt us blocks our vision and impedes the healing flow in our own lives. In his novel *A Separate Peace* John Knowles says, "Wars are not made by generations, but by something blind in the human heart."[23] He might have said that the whole tragedy of broken human relationships is caused by such blindness. Not until we learn to see our fellow human beings through the eyes of forgiveness can the well-springs of healing be released, both for the forgiver and the forgiven.

For some people, however, the most difficult task of forgiveness will not be that of forgiving others, but of forgiving themselves. In our discussion of the Realization period in Chapter One, we noted that guilt is among the most common emotions associated with grief. But guilt can extend well beyond regrets for things that happened during the period immediately surrounding our loss. The grief experience has a way of calling our whole life into question. We may have the sensation of seeing our life "pass before our eyes," as allegedly happens when people face physical death. This adds another painful dimension to our grieving, as we are "broken open" to review the wider scope of our life and possibly re-experience long-repressed sources of guilt.

A beautiful narrative about a person who found the pathway to self-acceptance is found in St. Luke's Gospel. It begins as follows:

> One of the Pharisees asked Jesus to eat with him, and he went into the Pharisee's house and took his place at the table. And a woman in the city, who was a sinner, having learned that he was eating in the Pharisee's house, brought an alabaster jar of ointment. She stood behind him at his feet, weeping, and began to bathe his feet with her tears and to dry them with her hair. Then she continued kissing his feet and anointing them with the ointment. Now when the Pharisee who had invited him saw it, he said to himself, "If this man were a prophet, he would have known who and what kind of woman this is who is touching him—that she is a sinner." (7:36-39 NRSV)

Sometimes the parts of a story which are *not* told are the most important, for they leave us with unanswered questions through which to enter the event ourselves. Who was this woman who comes into a dinner party from the streets and upsets the host? What had she done that caused her to be labeled a "sinner"? Almost certainly, St. Luke intends us to understand that she was a prostitute. An especially intriguing question is, why is the woman crying? What had happened to cast her into grief?

To appropriate this story we must set a bit of background. In our culture, for someone to come into a private home off the street would be alarming, and we would probably call the police. In Palestinian culture of that day, it was commonplace.

Doors were left open, and people wandered in and out. Beggars might ask for a handout. Strollers might stop for a while and listen to an interesting discussion. So it was not unusual for a stranger to come inside the house. At more formal dinners people reclined on couches, with their feet away from the table, and that is how the woman in the story could reach Jesus' feet.

While it was not odd for a *stranger* to appear at the dinner, the problem was this woman was not really a stranger. Evidently, she was rather well known, in fact, and her reputation always preceded her. She knew that she was taking a great risk to enter the home of a Pharisee, of all people. Pharisees were people who came home and washed merely because they had bumped against the common folk in the market place. Imagine what they would do if they inadvertently touched *this* woman! The woman knew, therefore, that she was most unwelcome in this particular house and might be humiliated and ejected. Why would she risk so much in order to reach Jesus?

I believe the woman came weeping that evening because she had already met Jesus. Maybe as he entered the village that day, she was slinking in the shadows along a side street, curious to get a look at him. And maybe he had stopped, where other "respectable" folk would have pretended not to see her. And maybe it was only a look he gave her, an incredible depth of accepting love, such as she had never before encountered. Perhaps there were not even words, but just a sudden inescapable awareness that she could have a different kind of life than the one she had.

Maybe for the first time in her broken life, she realized somehow that there really was something called forgiveness. Maybe in Jesus' eyes she saw a compassion that said, "Your past and all that has happened is no excuse. There is a beautiful person behind the outward appearance, yearning to be born. You are not trapped by your sins the way you think you are. You are not imprisoned and controlled by the old chains of your failures. You can have a new life." It was then that the woman knew that this man was unlike so many others she had known. She had basically known two kinds: the ones who exploited her and the ones who condemned her. Both were destructive. Neither offered hope. Neither kind loved her.

Perhaps it was only later in the day that she began to weep. It all began to sink in—the incredible possibility that her life really could be different. Hope began to well up within her. The awful core of shame that she carried deep within began to melt. Someone—just one person—had touched her with love, and she began to see herself in a different light. She was a person! Someone had actually looked at her with eyes of pure love. That meant that she was not a hopeless mistake after all. And the tears began, mingling seemingly opposite emotions, as tears often do. Some were grieving tears for all that she had missed in life, and some were tears of joy because there was a future for her after all.

At some point that day she resolved to find this Jesus, if only to thank him. That evening she searched the village for him and finally located him having dinner with his friends at the house of Simon the Pharisee. Her heart must have almost failed her. Of all places in town, she would be the least welcome here, but she risked it anyway.

From this point on the story is full of irony and paradox. Simon the "righteous" man watches the whole scene of her anointing Jesus' feet, and draws one simple conclusion. This Jesus is a phony. If he were so prophetic and insightful, he would certainly know what kind of woman this is who is weeping over him. That is the great irony. Jesus knows exactly who she is. But poor Simon doesn't know who anybody is. First, he doesn't know who the woman is, and cannot see the person made in God's image, shamed into darkness and fear, and longing for life and freedom. Then, he certainly doesn't know who Jesus is, but can only conclude that Jesus is ignorant or fraudulent or both, because he doesn't recoil from this "contaminated" woman.

Worst of all, Simon doesn't know who he himself is—a person just like the woman, broken and needy, if only he could let his defenses down and see it. He too holds a person trapped inside, frightened that he is not good enough. But instead of opening up to his inner hurt and need, he conceals it even from himself, with a rigid system of religious rule-keeping. This way he can always look good, to himself and to others. Jesus of course sees right through him to the real person inside.

This story is about the incredible mystery and power of forgiveness. Simon the Pharisee and the sinful woman are prototypes. The "righteous" one whom we might expect to be closest to God is the least able to receive God's love. The one whom we would think has the least spiritual depth turns out to have the most. She goes her way with a whole new relationship with God. Or as Jesus put it, "Your sins are forgiven. Your faith has saved you. Go in peace."

We may not see ourselves as trapped in Pharisaism or prostitution; yet self-righteousness is a common defense against our inner misgivings, and debasement of our self-worth is an almost universal malady. So the story is about us too. It is about how we come to be healed by the power of unconditional love, which enables self-acceptance. When that happens, then we too hear those incomparable words, "Go in peace. The real you doesn't have to be cut off from life anymore." We, like the grieving woman, can learn what Rokelle Lerner has aptly expressed: "I recognize that there is a statute of limitations on past errors. I do not have to pay and pay forever... I need to forgive myself for all the harm I have done to me."[24]

The inability to forgive ourselves is part of the way that we negate and neglect the child within. It is crucial to our Recovery that we learn to become our own nurturing parent. We commonly carry into adult life a relationship with our inner child that reflects the inadequate or even abusive parenting styles that we learned in early childhood. In this pattern the adult, nurturing side of us remains stifled, so that our conscious life is dominated by an incessant dialogue between our judgmental, critical-parent nature and our child within. The parent voices are constantly censuring our feelings, creative urges, and our struggle for differentiation. The beleaguered child within us, when under the domination of the critical parent faculty, has only two basic choices: to conform or to rebel. A vast amount of adult behavior can be understood from this perspective, as we see persons acting either from motives of long-repressed anger and rebellion, or from shame-bound conformity and humiliation.

What is missing here is an adequately developed, mature adult function. The "Adult" within us must be brought to sufficient maturity to be able to mediate between the critical faculty and the hurting child. The adult function calls upon our experience, education, and accumulated wisdom to assess and reject the unreasonable and abusive harangues of our inner censorious parent. This is the issue that is activated in grief processes which evoke unhealthy and inappropriate guilt. In the pain of loss, the child within may be unable to muster even its usual defenses against the abusive inner parent and, hence, the suffering is compounded by excessive guilt.

We may be placed in touch with childhood pain from our family of origin, as we remember ways in which we were neglected, abused, or abandoned. We may reach our "shame core," in John Bradshaw's compelling phrase, where as children we banished from awareness our fear, not just of making mistakes (guilt), but of *being* a mistake (shame). We may also feel compelled to re-examine moral failures of the past which have long been too threatening to face.

More than anything, however, our more immediate loss may simply trigger an awareness of *all* that we feel we have missed in life—our whole basket of broken dreams, unfulfilled goals, and lost ideals. With this added dimension, our grief may at times seem to take on quite overwhelming proportions. Now it becomes crucial to our emotional and spiritual health to form a new relationship with the inner self. We must find a new depth of self-acceptance, whereby we learn to cherish our own life-story, a journey which has never happened before and never will be repeated in all of history. It becomes imperative that we "grieve" our whole story, as well as specific losses, so that it can be woven into a higher order of meaning than we have envisioned before.

In Arthur Miller's play *After the Fall*, the character Holga speaks of how we come to a place in life where we know that we must bend down and kiss the "idiot child" in our arms, a symbol of the brokenness of life:

> *And for a long time after I had the same dream each night—that I had a child; and even in the dream I saw that the child was my life; and it was an idiot. And I wept, and a hundred times I ran away, but each time I came back it had the same dreadful face. Until I thought, if I could kiss it, whatever in it was my own, perhaps I could rest. And I bent to its broken face, and it was horrible... but I kissed it.* [25]

This is a trenchant metaphor to say that we ultimately must recognize the absurdity that pervades every life story. We must open ourselves to grieve our cosmic, existential pain that is part of the human saga.

When we finally embrace the broken Child within we are standing at the threshold of the great healing, which is part of what religious faith has traditionally meant by the concept of "reconciliation." We will never finally be healed as long as we reject our life for its brokenness and imperfection. Eventually, true healing leads to a new acquaintance with the real Self within and an acceptance that much in our story does not "make sense." Despite the idiot child in our arms, our unique Selfhood bears God's image, and it is holy.

Sooner or later Recovery requires us to discover the all-important truth that we have to become our own parent. No one else will ever be able to serve in this role. From our adult, nurturing faculty, we say to our child within, "No matter how you have been treated before, I will never again abandon, neglect, ignore or abuse you. I will always be there for you. You are forgiven and loved unconditionally."

To summarize, forgiveness is not the same as approving of what someone has done to us, or just forgetting about it, or steeling oneself not to feel hurt, or acting as if it doesn't matter. Forgiveness is the extension of good will to others, even if they have hurt us, because we have learned to accept not only their brokenness, but also our own. Not to forgive is essentially to claim perfection for oneself, and that puts us in a false and untenable position with our fellow human beings.

Jesus said that we shall receive forgiveness in the same measure that we give it, because he knew that refusing to forgive is the same as refusing to look at our own brokenness and failure. It is to stand in a hopelessly self-righteous place from which no growth is possible. That is why he insisted that being *forgiving* is a pre-requisite to being *forgiven*.

Chapter Three

Childhood and
a Lesser God

O Jesus, keeper of all lost things, walk to me across these impossible waters. I offer you today my lost loves—those people whom I once treasured but with whom I have since suffered the pain of separation. I ask you to gather up a few redeeming moments of these loves of mine and save them for all eternity when we will be united again in an embrace which will never end. On that day we will betray each other no more. Forgive us for all the pain we've inflicted on each other in our blindness and immaturity. Give me the wisdom to get on with the beautiful business of life and not cling to my lost loves. Amen.

—Sister Macrina Wiederkehr[26]

Father, if the hour has come to make the break, help me not to cling, even though it feels like death. Give me the inward strength of my Redeemer, Jesus Christ, to lay down this bit of life and let it go, so that I and others may be free to take up whatever new and fuller life you have prepared for us, now and hereafter. Amen.

—Bishop John V. Taylor[27]

In the Gospel stories, Jesus anticipates his death and tries to prepare his followers for the time of his departure from the earthly scene. Predictably, this precipitates in the disciples a profound grief process, as they face the loss of the most important relationship in their lives. They are thrust into what is often called "anticipatory grief." In one familiar passage, Jesus seems to speak all too optimistically about his disciples as he says to them, "And you know the way to the place where I am going." (John 14:4 NSRV. See also 16:7.) Thomas ventures to correct the Master, in what is surely one of the most forlorn statements in the Gospels. He says, "Lord, we do not know where you are going. How can we know the way?" Thomas' words could be paraphrased to say,

> *Lord, because we don't know where you're going, we don't know where we're going. We don't know which direction to take without you. We had all our hopes pinned on you. You keep saying that it is better for us if you go away, but that doesn't make sense. We don't know what to do without you. Why are you leaving us like this?*

Surely Thomas is voicing a feeling that every one of us has when we realize that something of great value is being taken from us. We do not understand why it has to be, and we do not see how we are going to survive the loss. At such times we are likely to find ourselves struggling with the issue of where God is in it all.

The hour of grief is likely to thrust us into emotional and spiritual regression, where we encounter once again a more primal level of spirituality. It is rooted in our childhood. It is not wrong or shameful to find this within us, for it is, I believe, a universal experience. It can be partly a result of inadequate Christian education, partly a reflection of our "adapted child," but also reflects the limited capacity we had as children to understand God.

James W. Fowler has done pioneering work on the stages of faith development, drawing upon the work of Piaget, Kohlberg, and Erickson. He outlines seven stages of growth, the second of which, Mythic-Literal, is normally traversed in pre-adolescent years.[28] However, says Fowler, we may find it still dominant in adolescents and adults.[29] In this childhood stage one takes on "the stories, beliefs and observances that symbolize belonging to his or her community. Beliefs are appropriated with literal interpretations, as are moral rules and attitudes. Symbols are taken as one-dimensional and literal in meaning."[30] Failing to move beyond this stage, says Fowler, "can result in an over controlling, stilted perfectionism or 'works righteousness' or in their opposite, an abasing sense of badness embraced because of mistreatment, neglect or the apparent disfavor of significant others."[31] Since remnants of the early stages of faith development remain in most persons, it is not surprising to find a more primitive spirituality evoked by severe grief, because of our tendency to regress in times of crisis.

This early level of faith manifests itself in at least three kinds of feelings that tend to linger long past childhood:

First, we wish that someone would make our decisions for us, always telling us what to do, and taking away the scary risks of living and choosing. At one time in life, this was appropriate. Our parents or caretakers did much of this for us, because we were children, and could not do it for ourselves.

Second, we wish that someone would always affirm us— tell us that we were okay, always reassure us when our poor ego has gotten battered, when we have been deeply rejected, or when we have failed at something. How nice that would be! At one time in our lives our parents, if they were capable and available, often could do that for us appropriately. We were dependent upon them at that age for this kind of support.

Third, our childhood faith wishes that someone would protect us from the pain, danger, and sadness of life, making sure that we never got hurt, and that no bad things ever happen to good people. Once again, when we were little children our parents often could do this for us, shielding us as much as possible from harm's way.

As we grow into the realization that life is more complex than our childhood faith can accommodate, we have to face the fact that this early spirituality will not sustain us in our adult life. Confronting the need to give up our less mature spirituality can be very frightening, and we may feel a powerful temptation to retreat at that point. Sometimes people enter a fortress of rigid and unquestioned doctrine, and spend their energies shooting arrows at those who confront or question them in any way. That is how primitive spirituality works when it fails to mature. Peter Pan, the boy who refused to grow up, may be a charming childhood fantasy, but he is not exactly the ideal of mature Christian discipleship.

The story of Jesus' final departure from his disciples, described traditionally as the "Ascension," can be seen as a kind of paradigm of the growth experience that is required of us in grief. Very commonly, the grief journey constitutes a summons to move beyond childish dependency upon something (spouse, friend, institution, or "God," for example) which we hoped would always accomplish for us those three wonderful-sounding things outlined above. In the story of the Ascension we see that Jesus, the supreme image of authentic spirituality, does not treat us as dependent children, so that we never have to mature spiritually. That is why Jesus kept saying to the disciples (and, of course, to modern listeners also): "It is better for you if I go away. I will no longer be with you in this visible, tangible form that invites you to remain dependent on me and never have to find your *own* life, your *own* selfhood, your *own* strength. As an authentic Higher Power, I will be with you always, but only in the way of a mature parent, teacher, or mentor, who sustains, nurtures and supports, but does not dominate, control, or stifle *your* self-development."

Every effective parent or parent-figure knows this delicate balance, which is the only matrix in which healthy human beings can be created. We must support children in every appropriate way, but not become a crutch so their legs never grow strong. That is what Jesus' ascension was about and why it was necessary. It was the great transition to a kind of relationship which is beyond childhood dependency. It is a call to a higher spirituality than would have been possible if he had remained with us in some tangible form.

In the first of what are called the "resurrection appearances," one of the grieving women at the tomb recognizes Jesus and is overcome with emotion. In what seems at first a mystifying statement, Jesus says to her, "Do not *cling* to me,

Mary. I have not yet ascended to the Father." (John 20:17) If we decode this language, it may be seen as a message to all recovering people who wish that some Magic Person would come to us in a physical, tangible form that we could touch and control. The message in the Ascension experience, though not always welcome to us in our pain, is nonetheless essential to our healing. It says to us: "Do not cling to me, nor to anything external, in the dependent spirituality of childhood. I must ascend (you must let go) in order that *you* may ascend to a higher spirituality, which calls forth the unique self within you that the Creator had in mind from all eternity."

A grief crisis thus may expose within us an unresolved conflict between our primitive faith-response and our more mature theology. While our "heads" have developed fairly adult beliefs through study and experience, our inner child has continued to relate to God at a more simplistic level. In my first major grief experience, the birth of our handicapped child, it never occurred to me to question God, or to regard God as in any way the "cause" of this sad event. In fact, I shall never forget the words of one physician who straightened up from an examination of our child and said to my wife and me, "You must understand that there is no *reason* why this happened." I understood what he meant and appreciated his kindness. He was trying to tell us that we had not caused it. I already knew that this was true, because we had done everything required in terms of pre-natal care. I simply attributed it to the randomness and mystery of the created order of things, not to anything that we parents or God had done or left undone.

With the loss of my marriage, however, it was a far different matter. Two contradictory things seemed to be happening simultaneously. First, after the trauma broke open my inner life, I began to experience emotional and spiritual growth. I seemed to be getting in touch with a flow of the Spirit that I had never known before. There was a developing, quiet certainty of who I was, and that I did not have to depend on others to affirm my being. I could see that a process of rebirth was underway. Prayer, worship, and ministry began to come alive in fresh and more creative ways.

At the same time, I felt myself thrust back to a more primitive spirituality, which was not consistent with the reasonably mature theological perspective that I consciously held. John Sanford and his mentor Fritz Kunkel have offered a detailed and perceptive analysis of this phenomenon in terms of what they call "the crisis of the ego."[32] Kunkel says, "The psychological development during the first half of the crisis can be described as *regression*. The rigid prejudices of the Ego are melting away under the increasing pressure of perilous circumstances, and earlier, more childlike valuations are revitalized."[33]

In my crisis experience, at times I felt abandoned by God and wondered if, after all, we are utterly alone in the universe. My sense of God's protective guidance and providence seemed to crumble. I thought of St. Teresa's comment to God after a painful experience in her life: "If this is how you treat your friends, I don't wonder that you have so few."

As a Christian, I had diligently and prayerfully sought direction before entering into my marriage twenty-one years earlier. In no experience of my life had I ever felt more certainty than that our marriage was the right thing. Through our years together, I came to rely upon the marriage as a kind of "proof" of my faith in God's guiding hand in my life.

Like everyone, I experienced life's disappointments and unfulfilled dreams. Sorrow for our little girl's severe disabilities ran deep, but things always seemed more than compensated by a marriage relationship that gave life meaning and purpose. In the face of all of life's setbacks, there always stood this one unassailable evidence of God's loving presence with me. I interpreted my seemingly secure marriage and my happy family as proof that God was caring for me and blessing my life.

My "Santa Claus" view of God from childhood believed that life operated according to a basic principle: good boys and girls are rewarded and bad boys and girls are punished. It is, of course, beautiful in its simplicity. Armed with this fundamental

leverage, we can control the life-process and manipulate God. I bought into this game at a very early age. I figured out that being good paid off (in my family environment), and so I played by the rules. It worked for a long time. (See the discussion of Job and the "deuteronomic theology" in Chapter Five.)

The Reverend William J. O'Malley's book, *Daily Prayers for Busy People*, contains a prayer that exposes the folly of this spiritual blind alley:

> *Living God, for a long time I tried to bribe you with my goodness, then to bargain with promises for reprieves, bartering my soul with you, instead of surrendering what was already yours.*[34]

Despite the message of the Book of Job and the Christian paradigm of the Cross, my Child did not *really* believe that bad things could happen to good people. But on that fateful August morning when my marriage ended, the theology of childhood came tumbling down. Being a "good boy" and living by the rules, was no longer working. God, or something, was allowing the destruction of my dearest treasure on earth, my marriage relationship. I knew that my Santa Claus God was dead; my storybook world was ended. I could see some serious theology lurking in the familiar nursery rhyme:

> *Humpty Dumpty sat on a wall,*
> *Humpty Dumpty had a great fall;*
> *All the kings horses,*
> *And all the king's men,*
> *Cannot put Humpty Dumpty together again.*

Like Humpty Dumpty, the spirituality of childhood was shattered forever.

Sanford and Kunkel argue that we have to be *forced* out of our original Ego-defense systems by crisis, since it is virtually impossible to muster the courage to *will* our way out:

If this were possible by mere will-power the shell and the egocentricity would not be what they are—the old fortifications against anguish and fear. They seem to us to be the walls behind which we suppose the tigers and lions wait ready to seize us if they could get out.... We unconsciously oppose the destruction of these walls—these egocentric fortifications—even though we are consciously trying to demolish them and to laugh at them as being obsolete, useless, and childish.[35]

This helps to explain why childhood spiritual formations often co-exist across many years with our considerably more sophisticated theological outlook. Edna St. Vincent Millay understood this when she wrote,

> *Pity me that the heart is slow to learn*
> *What the swift mind beholds at every turn.*[36]

In my own journey, it took a major grief-crisis to expose this "house divided against itself" within me.

About three weeks after the stunning news from my wife that she wanted to end our marriage, I had a very strange experience. It should go without saying that my pain, anxiety, and disorientation during these early days of Reaction were extremely intense, which made the event seem even more unexplainable. Though many people had shared with me as a pastor their "visions" and mystical encounters, I had virtually no experience with such things myself. I should like to add that on the occasion of this experience I was taking no medication and had ingested nothing alcoholic.

In the late evening I was having my usual time of meditation and prayer. Upon reaching the Confession in the prayers for evening, the words seemed to come alive, especially the part which says "We have not loved you with our whole heart." I began to realize that I had made my marriage the center of my life. I had "idolized" my wife both in the popular and the Old Testament senses of the word. I felt a burning sense of

what the Hebrew prophets must have meant by "idolatry": trying to find the meaning of one's life in some external source,
even though it may be something good in itself, rather than in
God, the True Center and Ground of our Being. I saw that
"addiction" and "co-dependency" are only our modern ways
of describing what the Old Testament warned about long ago
as linking one's life to "idols."

I knew that much in our marriage had been healthy, nurturing, and good, but now I began to face in myself the hurtful elements of relationship-addiction and dependency, which
also were present. I had sought life too much outside myself
through another person, rather than in the only place where it
truly exists: the Real Self within.[37] Later a statement by Agnes
Repplier, quoted by Melody Beattie in her fine work,
Codependent No More, would take its place in my canon of personal "scripture": "It is not easy to find happiness in ourselves,
and it is not possible to find it elsewhere."[38]   And I remembered that St. Augustine had reflected this same fundamental
insight 1,500 years earlier when he asked, "How can I be close
to God, when I am far from myself?"

As the "vision" continued it seemed as if the whole earth
shifted on its axis. An image formed of a great stone or boulder rolling down into exactly the place that had been hewn out
for it. It rolled into place with a thunderous sound. The great
stone now rested at the center of an open space with a brilliant
light shining down upon it, forming a large circle of light. I
looked across this intensely lighted area and saw my wife
standing just outside the circle, slightly in the shadows.

It seemed clear to me what the "vision" meant. I saw that
God as I knew him in Jesus Christ now had to occupy the center of my life and nothing else, and I resolved that how ever
long I lived it would always be so. During the time that these
images pervaded my consciousness, a hymn fragment kept
running through my mind: "The dearest idol I have
known...." I could not recover any more of it at that point.

The "vision" finally faded and I finished my prayers. I fell
asleep for an hour or so and then awakened not long after mid-

night. I was bathed in a feeling of calm and peacefulness such as I had never experienced before nor have felt again since that night. It was utterly beyond description in language. I was floating effortlessly in a pool of water which was exactly the right temperature, not too hot, not too cold. A golden light was all around, but this light was not at all harsh and did not hurt the eyes or burn in any way. It was different from the more bluish light which had encircled the stone. The pool seemed to be hewn out of a rock that went to the center of the earth, or the core of the universe, and it felt like a place to be secure forever.

I remained awake for the remainder of the night. I wanted to stay there for always and was afraid that if I went to sleep the experience would go away and I would never recover it. Through the night the hymn fragment continued to play in the back of my mind: "The dearest idol I have known...." With the coming of the morning light, the experience gradually faded away, though for several more hours I felt a great peace within. During the morning as I naturally tried to reflect on what this whole experience could mean, I mistakenly thought at first that I had been carried across the raging river of my pain to some miraculous victory over grief. How far from the truth that proved to be!

In many reflective moments since that strange night I have in fact sometimes felt angry that I was given a taste of such unspeakable serenity, but have never found it again and do not know the path that would lead to it. The early part of the vision about the boulder rolling into place within the circle of light remains clear, however. Its meaning was reinforced early that morning when I suddenly remembered the old hymn from which the fragment had come. It is entitled "O for a closer walk with God," by the English hymn-writer William Cowper, and the fourth verse reads:

> *The dearest idol I have known,*
> *whate'er that idol be,*
> > *help me to tear it from thy throne,*
> > *and worship only thee.*

An excellent study by Gerald G. May entitled *Addiction and Grace* has provided much additional insight as I have continued to try to interpret this experience. May says:

> *For me, the energy of our basic desire for God is the human spirit, planted within us and nourished endlessly by the Holy Spirit of God. In this light, the spiritual significance of addiction is not just that we lose freedom through attachment to things, nor even that things so easily become our ultimate concerns. Of much more importance is that we try to fulfill our longing for God through objects of attachment. For example, God wants to be our perfect lover, but instead we seek perfection in human relationships and are disappointed when our lovers cannot love us perfectly.*[39]

Moreover, there seems to be no time limit on how long our addictions/idolatries can endure. For me it was half a lifetime.

> *For many of us, freedom of choice means that our longing for the true God remains submerged within us for months, years, or even decades at a time, while our conscious energies seek satisfaction elsewhere… Often it is not until the momentum brings us to some point of existential despair, some rock bottom, some* impasse, *that we become capable of beginning to reclaim our true desire.*[40]

The breakup of every idolatry requires the mourning of our loss. "Only then, when we have completed the grieving over our lost attachment," says May, "will we breathe the fresh air of freedom with appreciation and gratitude."[41]

The spiritual growth which results in this freedom, however, is not without cost. Fritz Kunkel in his book *Creation Continues* has warned of this quite forcefully:

> *Wherever the Spirit of Christ appears, the historical situation becomes clear, the unconscious relationship between*

relatives and friends is brought to consciousness; sham love is recognized as hatred, and sham morality is unmasked as selfishness. Invisible weapons become visible; where we expected the kiss of allegiance, we get the snarl of an enemy. Primitive confidence and childlike faith break down. The crisis is there and for a moment we wish that the messengers of the Light had never come to show us the truth—until experience reveals that it is this very truth that sets us free. [42]

This may help to explain what Kierkegaard meant when he spoke of a paradoxical experience that he called "the dizziness of freedom."

We also may be pulled away from our new freedom by the desire to make even God into a new addiction, placing God into some doctrinal, moralistic, liturgical, or denominational framework. But, continues Dr. May, "there can be no addiction to the true God, because God refuses to be an object... Therefore, the journey homeward does not lead toward new, more sophisticated addictions. If it is truly homeward, it leads toward liberation from idolatrous addiction altogether. For most of us, this is a lifelong process."[43] Perhaps my "vision" was some kind of signpost, pointing the way toward home. As I reflected on the vision and the loss of my marriage, some words of Christina Georgina Rossetti from "Monna Innominata" seemed somewhat fitting:

> *I love, as you would have me, God the most;*
> *Would lose not Him, but you, must one be lost.*

The issue of facing our idolatries is powerfully illustrated by an exchange that took place one time in Jerusalem between Jesus and his disciples. (Luke 21:5-19) At that point in history the Herodian kings had been in the process of refurbishing and embellishing the temple for almost 50 years. The east face of the temple was probably constructed of white marble, with lots of gold inlay. The temple was Israel's pride and joy, the great symbol of their cultural and spiritual heritage.

One day as Jesus and the disciples drew near the temple its gold and marble must have appeared especially magnificent in the sunlight. The disciples were awestruck before its gleaming beauty, and they commented on it to Jesus. "Yes, it's beautiful," we can imagine him saying. "It is a great symbol of our long journey of faith. But the day will come when not one stone of it will be left upon another. It will all be thrown down." The impact of what Jesus said can hardly be overstated. The disciples were dumbfounded. He was striking at the very heart of traditional faith. Probably the only thing comparable to it in our day would be desecrating the flag!

Not only was the temple the supreme symbol of Israel's national pride, but it was also regarded as a means of protection. A long-standing piece of popular piety held that God would never let anything happen to his temple. No matter how bad things got under the Romans, the temple was always there as a reminder that Israel was superior and would somehow be protected. By saying that the temple was only a temporal, finite creation, therefore, Jesus attacked one of the society's most cherished illusions. Far more than just a beloved building, the temple also stood for a whole belief system. It supported Israel's fantasy that she was ultimately invulnerable and that God was committed to preserving her forever as a nation.

This bit of history, however, is only prelude to what is important in the story. The issue Jesus raised with his disciples reaches across the ages to us also: what can we count on? In what do our true hope and security lie? A grief journey often confronts us with the realization that it is not where we thought—in the gleaming, beautiful projections that we create in our own imagination. How quickly they can be brought down, not one stone left upon another! How swiftly the Roman legions can sweep through our lives leveling what we thought was inviolable!

The disciples were profoundly disturbed when Jesus undermined their conception of what was really trustworthy. They wanted to know what they could do and how they could prepare for the day of loss and destruction. Jesus did not promise that they would escape the pain of earthly tribulation. He warned that the human temples which we think are so secure can come tumbling down at any time. Then, as he predicted, the warring empires within us will rage, and our world will seem shaken by earthquakes. We will feel the inner famine of our souls, which we may have tried to avoid for a long time. We will feel the interrogation of our innermost heart, as if we are being dragged before magistrates and kings. (See Luke 21:9-19)

This brief story carries a profound question for everyone who is thrust into loss and grief: How are we to face the apocalypses in our lives, when so much that we had built upon lies in ruins? One of faith's hardest tasks is to learn that this is the first step in the healing of every human soul. It is one of the deepest mysteries of the spiritual life: until we are broken we cannot be healed. Until the walls of our temples, the places of worship that we erect in place of God, come tumbling down, we cannot see the true God. Until our defensive structures begin to fall, we cannot realize our total dependence on God and thus cannot know that joyous liberation which the Bible calls grace. (See Step One of the twelve-step recovery programs.)

A contemporary song written by Brown Bannister, Chris Christian, and Amy Grant speaks perceptively of the deepening of our spirituality through the loss of our poor earthly idolatrous "temples":

> *I had laid some mighty plans,*
> *Thought I held them in my hands,*
> *Then my world began to crumble all away.*
> *I tried to build it back again,*
> *I couldn't bear to see it end,*
> *How I hurt to know You wanted it that way.*

> *Long before my plans were made*

I know a master plan was laid
With a power that superseded my control.
And if that truth could pierce my heart
I wouldn't wander from the start
Trying desperately to make it on my own.

(Chorus)
And I'm so glad, glad to find the reason
That I'm happy-sad You've torn it all away.
And I'm so glad, though it hurts to know I'm leaving
Everything I ever thought that I would be.
Once I held it in my hand,
It was a kingdom made of sand,
But now You've blown it all away.
I can't believe that I can say I'm glad.[44]

Jesus doesn't say that the apocalyptic times will not come to his people. He offers no magic formula for escaping them. Rather, he talks about how to find life on the other side of them. He makes the incredible promise that when we are bound to him, not a hair of our head will perish, and that even when our kingdoms of sand are blown away, by holding on to him we will gain our lives.

Chapter Four

He Has Heard the Sound of My Weeping

I asked God for all things, that I might enjoy life.
I was given life, that I might enjoy all things.
I got nothing that I asked for, but everything I had hoped for.
Almost despite myself, my unspoken prayers were answered.

—Anonymous

I grow weary because of my groaning; every night I drench my bed
and flood my couch with tears. My eyes are wasted with grief and
worn away because of all my enemies. Depart from me, all evildoers,
for the Lord has heard the sound of my weeping. The Lord has heard
my supplication; the Lord accepts my prayer.

—Psalm 6:6-9

One of the areas most deeply affected by grief is our praying. It hardly seems legitimate, therefore, to discuss the grief journey without examining its relationship to prayer. Some years ago, the late Theodore P. Ferris well described a critical moment that comes to virtually every human being:

There is bound to come a time, sooner or later, when you
want something desperately, and you know that you cannot
get it by your own efforts. Someone you love is sick and you
want him to get well; you may be sick yourself and want to

get well; or you are out of a job and you want one; or you have lost your grip on life and you want to get it back. When that time comes, you pray and ask God to give you the thing you so desperately want…. Whether you are in the habit of praying or not, when a time like this comes, you will pray almost instinctively, simply because you cannot help it. You may not pray according to any liturgical form or pattern, but you will turn in your helplessness to whatever gods there be and ask for help.[45]

After such prayers, there occur those astonishing times when one receives almost exactly what was asked, perhaps with breathtaking swiftness. Many other times, however, we do not seem to receive any kind of answer except the silence of what may feel like an infinite void. This can be the occasion for very serious spiritual conflict, as doubt mounts a massive attack upon faith. We enter what the saints and mystics have called "the dark night of the soul."

If we have been carrying a childhood view of God which is now profoundly shaken, the spiritual crisis is further complicated. Our prayer life is one of the most accurate barometers of the theology that *actually* controls our spirituality, beneath the rational level. In crisis, a more primitive theology may emerge, as we have discussed in the previous chapter, because we are thrust once again into that frightful vulnerability which we often felt as a child. Our praying may begin to reflect once again the level of our more simplistic childhood faith.

Prayer for the child is essentially magical. A hallmark of childhood thinking is that the demarcation between the real and the imaginary is not fully developed. For children, prayer is often a kind of incantation, by which they try magically to obtain the things they desire, but know they cannot obtain by their own limited strength. Much of our childhood praying is like writing letters to Santa Claus.

This is not entirely unlike what Elizabeth Kubler-Ross has termed the "bargaining" stage of grief. At some time in life almost everyone has attempted some kind of "trade agreement" with the Almighty. We may have promised, for example, that if we or someone we love can recover, or if something we desperately want can come to pass, we will never miss church again, will give generously of our material goods, enter a religious profession, or whatever.

The theological premise behind bargaining and Santa Claus praying is of course that God controls and orders all events in exact conformity to his wishes. (We will examine the difficulties with this perspective more fully in the next chapter.) Like that fateful day when we learned there was no Santa Claus, we also reach a spiritual crossroads when we realize that this kind of prayer does not work. Then we face a fundamental decision whether to search out a deeper spirituality or to relegate faith to the worn out toys of childhood and give up prayer forever.

The primitive level of spirituality is powerfully reinforced in our day by the popular media religionists who constantly promote a kind of magical faith. If we will only adopt certain premises or practices, they proclaim, we will enjoy health, prosperity, and happiness in abundance. This insidious doctrine is responsible for a vast amount of guilt and confusion, because it implies that when we suffer we have brought it upon ourselves, because we did not follow the prescribed faith formulas. It is vital to genuine Recovery and to all authentic spirituality that this egregious heresy be exposed and that we be enabled to move to the far different kind of faith expounded by Jesus Christ and the whole Biblical heritage.

The prayer of Jesus in the Garden of Gethsemane is the clue to the meaning of genuine prayer. It lays to rest forever our manifold idolatries and childhood gods. Dag Hammarskjöld grasped the centrality of the Gethsemane experience in the life of faith. A very devout man, Hammarskjöld often quoted St. John of the Cross, who said "Faith is the marriage of God and the Soul." But faith, Hammarskjöld discovered, is often born in the dark night of the soul—a time "so dark that we may not even look for faith."

It is the "night in Gethsemane when the last friends left you have fallen asleep, all the others are seeking your downfall, and *God is silent*, as the marriage is consummated."[46]

As he faced the agony of cruel suffering and death Jesus prayed in Gethsemane, "Father, if it be possible let this cup pass from me; nevertheless, not my will but thine be done." If we allow these words to become the norm of prayer, we see very quickly that prayer is something much greater than simply trying to get God to give us what we want.

1. The first part of Jesus' Gethsemane prayer affirms that there is indeed a legitimate place for petition. Jesus asks for something. He was not a masochist. Indeed, his exuberance for life was so great that his detractors accused him of being a glutton, a wine-bibber, a party-goer. Jesus asked if he could save his life, and be spared the horrible suffering and death that he saw ahead of him.

This kind of prayer will happen, as Theodore Ferris said, almost instinctively, when we stand at those extremities of life and our own strength is exhausted. It will rise spontaneously within us, when in the depths of the abyss we face the stark limits of our finitude. This part of Jesus' prayer shows us that it certainly is not wrong to ask for fulfillment of our needs and hopes. However, the remainder of the prayer shows us that this is not prayer's deepest purpose.

2. The second part of Jesus' cry in Gethsemane brings us to the essence of prayer. When we have studied all the kinds, styles, and forms of prayer, when we have read the countless volumes written about the techniques of prayer, when we have heard the long history of the amazing results of prayer, we will still have to return here if we are really to understand it. Jesus prayed, "Nevertheless, not my will, but yours be done." With that, he centered his life in the Father. He surrendered his human level of insight to a higher wisdom. He took his stand in the "Kingdom of God," or rulership of the Father, about which he had taught so fervently. He handed over his human destiny to the Father's ultimate purpose. That spiritual action is the absolute heart of genuine prayer.

This gradual movement into the meaning of prayer is reflected in Dag Hammarskjöld's spiritual journey. In the introduction to *Markings*, W. H. Auden has recounted some of Hammarskjöld's growth-struggle. As late as 1952, long after he had attained international fame, the Secretary-General was still troubled by depression and sometimes beset by a powerful death wish. Auden says:

> *Long before he discovered a solution, Hammarskjöld knew exactly what his problem was—if he was not to go under, he must learn how to forget himself and find a calling in which he could forget himself—and knew that it was not in his own power to do this. The transition from despair over himself to faith in God seems to have been a slow process, interrupted by relapses. Two themes came to preoccupy his thoughts. First, the conviction that no man can do properly what he is called upon to do in this life unless he can learn to forget his ego and act as an instrument of God. Second, that for him personally, the way to which he was called would lead to the Cross, i.e., to suffering, worldly humiliation, and the physical sacrifice of his life.*[47]

No amount of rhetorical eloquence, liturgical propriety, or emotional intensity will turn our efforts into prayer without this fundamental act of centering in God. On the other hand, the most halting, broken, inarticulate cry accompanied by this action is transmuted directly into prayer at its deepest level.

The act of God-centering is the *sine qua non* of all that deserves to be called by the name of prayer. St. Paul certainly understood this when he said "Likewise the Spirit helps us in our weakness; for we do not know how to pray as we ought, but the Spirit himself intercedes for us with sighs too deep for words." (Romans 8:26 NRSV) The King James Version is more powerful here: "with groanings too deep for utterance." St. Paul's insight is reflected movingly by Nathan Kollar in his book *Songs of Suffering*. Sometimes, says Kollar, "The God we pray to does not seem to respond or to initiate any new consciousness. Praying is like singing down an empty hall: We hear only our own song.... We scream. And in the scream is the beginning of prayer."[48]

Jesus' parable of the Pharisee and the publican invites us to examine the roots of genuine prayer, where our screams and our "groans too deep for utterance" become our link with Healing Love (Luke 18:9-14). The story could be seen as an exposition of the words of Second Isaiah: "Thus says the high and lofty One who inhabits eternity, whose name is Holy, 'I dwell in the high and holy place and also with the one who has a contrite and humble spirit, to revive the spirit of the humble and to revive the heart of the contrite'." (57:15 NRSV) The Pharisee comes before God in the only way he has learned. It is exactly what most of us learned in early childhood. We come presenting our good, acceptable, outward self—our mask.

Jesus often cried out warnings to the Pharisees, saying "There is woe ahead for you, because you are hypocrites." The Greek word hypocrite means "actor." On the Greek stage, actors wore masks to indicate which role they were playing. Part of what sin means in the Bible is that we were all taught to be actors and wear our masks. The pride and self-congratulation which the Pharisee wore were his mask, a role he had learned to play. Long ago he had forgotten about the inner self that the mask was hiding. The mask was a cover for his deep-seated fear of facing his true self. If he did that, then he would have to see that he was a flawed, broken, and imperfect human being like everyone else, and his illusion of superiority would fall away. In John Bradshaw's terms, his "shame-core" would be exposed and he would have to face his inner misgivings about his own worth.

The story contains one particularly remarkable line. It says, "The Pharisee stood and prayed with himself." Sadly, his prayer was just a shallow utterance from his surface self, the "ego." Until the healing journey begins, that is the only part that we allow the world—and ourselves—to see. He couldn't really talk with God, because God is Truth and is found in our true self, the broken self that in our recovery we no longer have to banish from awareness.

What was different about the tax-collector? Why did Jesus draw such a strong contrast between him and the Pharisee, saying that the tax-collector went home "justified"—set right, no longer missing the mark? We dare not sentimentalize tax-collectors. Theirs was a dirty business. The Romans sold this job to the highest bidder and then allowed the person to extort all the taxes he could from his fellow-citizens. The nearest modern groups to whom we might compare them would be those involved in organized crime or drug-traffickers. They were generally cruel and despicable people.

Both the Pharisee and the tax-collector had missed the mark in life. They were both running from who they really were. There was only one difference. Something had happened to the tax-collector and his mask had been shattered. We don't know what that was. We only know that he had been thrust into the grief journey. Maybe he had lost something very precious—a child, a spouse, a friend, a dream. Somehow this loss had broken open his defenses and exposed to him his true inner life, how he had missed the mark. Whatever it was, the rationalizations he had employed for so long were shattered. There he stood, naked before the truth about his life, seeing himself as he really was.

He risked going to a place where he was utterly unwelcome, the temple. Jesus says that he stood afar off, perhaps in a dark corner, hiding behind a column. He dare not draw up close, for so despised was his class that he might even have been stoned. Who knows how long it had been since he had tried to utter a prayer? Maybe it was forty years before in synagogue school. All he could get out was, "God, be merciful to me, a sinner. God, I'm at the end of my little rope. I've missed the mark for so long, I don't know how to find my way back." And that, said Jesus, was real prayer. That day the tax-collector's whole life was turned around and he started the journey home.

The parable suggests that there are only two basic ways to pray: One is, clinging pathetically to our little ego-masks, which we were taught was all we dare show to God, to others, and to ourselves. The other is to come without our masks—poor, exposed, and vulnerable, with our whole being, knowing that God cannot heal what we do not bring. We believe that he will not reject anyone who kneels beside the tax-collector to pray, "Here I am, Lord, the real me, to tell my whole story. I have missed the way, but you know how to point me toward home."

Another of Jesus' parables is on the theme of persistence in prayer as a bulwark against losing heart in the midst of our suffering (Luke 18:1-8). A poor widow had suffered an injustice. To say "poor widow" was probably a redundancy in that day, because virtually all widows were poor. No social system existed to protect them—just the voluntary mercy of friends and relatives. What was the injustice? Maybe it was some injury perpetrated against one of her children, or perhaps it involved some hard-earned wages that she was due. Almost certainly, as a widow she was grieving over a lost future. She was struggling for survival. Her future lay in this unprincipled judge's hands, who evidently cared nothing about justice, much less mercy. Finally, however, he gave in and resolved her problem, not out of principle, but just to get her off his back. He simply got tired of her pestering him.

It is of course a parable of contrast, which was a teaching device that Jesus liked to use. The point is not that God is like the judge, so that we have to badger him into hearing our prayers, but the opposite: God is so *unlike* the judge that we need never lose heart in bringing our needs, our brokenness, and our hurt to him.

This parable reveals the relationship between prayer and "waiting upon the Lord," which we discussed earlier in the section on Realization (Chapter One). The widow is another one of the great spiritual "waiters" in the Biblical story. She waited and prayed with that active, hopeful, persistent expectancy, which is inseparable from what the Bible means by faith. In his book *A Passion for Truth*, Abraham Joshua Heschel describes well the goal of "waiting" prayer: "This is the task: in the darkest night to be certain of the dawn, certain of the power to turn a curse into a blessing, agony into a song... to go through Hell and to continue to trust in the goodness of God—this is the challenge and the way."[49]

The parable of the importunate widow leads rather naturally to one of the most vexing problems about prayer, which almost invariably confronts us in grief. It is the question of "unanswered" prayer. Why is so much that we ask for in prayer denied, or at least not granted in the time-frame that we would have desired? Let us consider two possible reasons:

1. In our brokenness and finitude we do not always know how to ask for what is best. The love of God, therefore, constrains God to deny requests that would be harmful to us. How many times have we looked back and realized that something we fervently prayed for, and thought we could not live without, would have been dreadfully wrong for us and might even have ruined our lives? Perhaps we asked for a certain job, or the success of a particular relationship, or acceptance into some group, which later insight revealed would have been a great mistake.

This only partially answers our questions about why we sometimes obtain our requests in prayer and sometimes do not. Certainly many things remain on our list of earnest desires, which we still deeply believe it would have been best for us to have received. We still may be far from understanding why so much pain and loss is required of us. We can see, however, that our praying, as our living, is done in partiality and relativity. We do not have absolute knowledge about anything, not even what is best in our own lives.

This theme is borne out in numerous traditional prayers, one of the clearest of which says:

Almighty God, to whom our needs are known before we ask, help us to ask only what accords with your will; and those good things which we dare not, or in our blindness cannot ask, grant us for the sake of your son Jesus Christ our Lord.

A similar note is sounded in this great old prayer:

Heavenly Father, you have promised to hear what we ask in the Name of your Son: Accept and fulfill our petitions, we pray, not as we ask in our ignorance, nor as we deserve in our sinfulness, but as you know and love us in your Son Jesus Christ our Lord.[50]

2. The second reason why our prayers cannot always be answered as we desire is that the growth we need would be short-circuited and the healing journey aborted. Parents who sent their children to school but shielded them from having to do homework and take exams would thwart the educational process. A music teacher who always exempted the pupil from practice or performance would produce no virtuosos. Codependent enablers who have a need to shield others from responsibility for their actions only perpetuate immaturity and unhealthy relationships. If we believe that life is a school for soul-making, then the application of these analogies is obvious. God could not fulfill our every desire or shield us from all of life's pain without robbing us of the essential conditions for spiritual growth.

Fritz Kunkel illustrated the importance of this understanding of prayer in a description of one of his clients:

Now we see that his demand was too superficial and its fulfillment would have been a pedagogical error, so to speak. The unconscious conflict with his sister, which persisted in the deeper layers of his personality, would never have been settled and his full independence would never have been developed, if his "symptoms" had disappeared before the deeper problem of his maturity had been disclosed. Character cannot be developed in any such evasive way. In such a case, therefore, one's prayer should be: "Help me to solve the problem which lies hidden beneath my shortcomings. Do not deliver me from these symptoms before I see what they mean."[51]

To expect God to operate at a level beneath even our human

wisdom is of course absurd, and yet our attempts to use prayer to manipulate God sometimes reflect this kind of expectation.

If prayer then is more than asking God to give us what we desire, what is its essential purpose? The answer is, we pray for the same reason that we attempt any other kind of communication: to establish and nurture a relationship. Genuine prayer is the centering of our life in God, as the Absolute Ground of all that has final claim upon us. This is what Jesus called "entering the Kingdom of God." In prayer we seek the Center of our existence, on which is founded our ultimate values, loyalties, and commitments—what Paul Tillich termed our "ultimate concern."

If prayer is indeed that link with the Infinite Reality that transcends us, then by its nature it will always remain mysterious and partially unexplainable. Often we experience in a direct and immediate way the *inner* transformation that is wrought by prayer. Much harder to comprehend is how prayer can affect the course of *external* events, as when we intercede for other people or ask for God's intervention in the world. One of the most astute comments on this intercessory dimension of prayer, commendable both in its simplicity and its humility, is attributed to the great Archbishop of Canterbury, William Temple: "I do not presume to understand the mystery of prayer," he said. "All I know is that when I stop praying, the 'coincidences' stop happening."

Our goal here has not been to offer a manual on prayer or fully explore its limitless power, but rather to address some of the issues that confront us most acutely in the grief journey. Trust in the efficacy of prayer is the heart of all spirituality. It is not too much to say that our Recovery ultimately will depend on our entering into the mystery of prayer. This is stated in the eleventh step of the Twelve-Step programs: "Sought through prayer and meditation to improve our conscious contact with God, *as we understood Him*, praying only for knowledge of His will for us and the power to carry that out."

Jesus' familiar words are often quoted as an encouragement to prayer:

> *Ask, and it will be given you; search, and you will find; knock, and the door will be opened for you... Is there anyone among you who, if your child asks for bread, will give a stone? Or if the child asks for a fish, will give a snake? If you then, who are evil, know how to give good gifts to your children, how much more will your Father in heaven give good things to those who ask him! (Matthew 7:7, 9-11 NRSV)*

As we have seen, however, this and similar statements of Jesus cannot possibly be interpreted to mean that we shall obtain everything that we ask for in prayer. Jesus himself did not. His plea that the bitter cup of suffering pass from him was not granted. In a few hours after raising this cry of the heart he was under the brutal lash and was carrying his own cross of cruel injustice to the Place of a Skull for execution with common criminals.

Note that in a parallel version of this saying, St. Luke has offered a more profound understanding of it and indeed has preserved the indispensable clue to its meaning. Instead of Matthew's promise of "good things," Luke's version says, "how much more will the heavenly Father give the *Holy Spirit* to those who ask him?" (Luke 11:13, emphasis added.) Matthew's version is more subject to the popular misinterpretation of prayer as magic, which we discussed earlier. Luke's wording better captures what we are calling the essence of prayer: while no prayer goes "unanswered," what we receive is more of God's Self, experienced as spiritual and emotional growth. This is not merely another of the "good things" of life, but is the highest gift of all.

Chapter Five

Something There Is
That Power Destroys

Hard it is, very hard,
To travel up the slow and stony road
To Calvary, to redeem mankind; far better
    To make but one resplendent miracle,
Lean through the cloud, lift the right hand of power,
And with a sudden lightening smite the world perfect.
Yet this was not God's way, Who had the power,
    But set it by, choosing the cross, the thorn,
The sorrowful wounds. Something there is, perhaps,
That power destroys in passing, something supreme,
    To whose great value in the eyes of God
That cross, that thorn, and those five wounds bear witness.

    —Dorothy L. Sayers[52]

Your pain is the breaking of the shell that
    encloses your understanding.
Even as the stone of the fruit must break, that
    its heart may stand in the sun, so must you know pain....
It is the bitter potion by which the physician
    within you heals your sick self....
And the cup he brings, though it burn your lips,
    has been fashioned of the clay which the Potter has
moistened with His own sacred tears.

    —Kahlil Gibran[53]

Every grief journey, to be successfully completed, must become a spiritual journey. As grief moves past initial shock and Reaction, the great issues of faith come alive in a far deeper way for the grieving person, particularly the question of whether there is ultimately any meaning in our suffering. We have to find an answer through discovering afresh the inner wells of spiritual strength. We have to re-define the Higher Power of the Universe, and our relationship to this ultimate Spiritual Reality.

In our discussion of the Realization phase of grief in Chapter One, we identified the problem of evil and innocent suffering as the single most troubling faith-question that people confront. It is what most often causes us to feel angry at God. Grief usually voices this in the form of the question, "Why did God let this happen to me?" As a pastor, I hear that difficult and painful question repeatedly, and I hear it in my own heart too. Before our faith can reach maturity, we have to come to grips with it.

On one occasion Jesus is told two stories of unjustified suffering and death. (Luke 13:1-6) In one case, some Galileans who had come to the temple to worship were slaughtered by Pontius Pilate's henchmen for some reason. Perhaps they were suspected of political disloyalty. The other story was about eighteen people, probably workmen building some kind of tower, who were killed when the structure accidentally fell on them.

Jesus, of course, knew about the common interpretation of such events in his day. Popular theology taught that bad things happen only to bad people, and conversely good things happen to good people. In other words, the things that happen are a working out of divine justice—a cosmic system of reward and punishment. If bad things happen to you, according to this viewpoint, you obviously did something to deserve it. On the other hand, if your life runs smoothly and happily, you are clearly being rewarded for your goodness.

This theory is especially prominent in the Old Testament book of Deuteronomy, and therefore scholars often call it "deuteronomic theology."[54] At least six hundred years before Jesus, this teaching provoked a literary and spiritual masterpiece, the Book of Job, which was written to refute the deuteronomic thesis. Even though Job represents a brilliant and valiant attempt, it evidently did not have much effect, because Jesus is still trying to counteract the doctrine centuries later.

Why is this theology so persistent? Why has it lasted thousands of years and is still going strong in many circles today? The answer seems to be that, first of all, it contains an element of truth, indeed an important element. Certainly, it does matter to our health and well-being how we live, what values we hold, and the basic attitudes we have. There is clearly a relationship between our happiness and our way of life. But this is only a part of the truth. To stretch it into a full explanation of human suffering is extremely cruel to suffering people who are victimized not by *their* wrongdoing, but that of others—the broken world around them.

Does anybody, for example, believe that children with AIDS contracted from a blood transfusion or from their parents are receiving justice for something that they as children have done? Can anybody believe that the people who are thrust out of a damaged jetliner to their death are worse people than the others who manage to remain in the plane and land safely? How could anyone endorse the idea that bystanders killed by gangs in drug-related shootings somehow deserve this fate? It seems clear that the first serious error that deuteronomic theology makes is that it overlooks the corporate nature of our life—how what we do affects each other—and assumes that sin is an individual matter.

There is a second powerful reason for the persistence of this doctrine: it protects us from having to face the fearful fact of life's randomness. There is simply an unexplainable, accidental dimension to life which seems to be built into the created order of things—the interaction between nature's freedom and nature's lawfulness. This means that much of what happens in life simply cannot be predicted and controlled, and few things make us more uneasy than facing that fact. The deuteronomic theology promises a way to retain control of life: do good and all will be well, while those who choose bad will get what they deserve. We may wish that life were that neatly controllable, but it isn't! God gave up that possibility when God invested the creation with freedom.

What is Jesus' response to the stories of human tragedy recounted in Luke 13? First, he flatly rejects the notion that the victims of the tragedies were worse than other people who suffered no such fate. He says that our encounters with pain and darkness are always a call to turn life around and enter more deeply into God's grace and love. That is what the word "repent" means, which Jesus uses in this passage. "Repentance" (Greek, *metanoia*) is an act of trust that our Higher Power will transform the tragic events of life into a richer and deeper life of the spirit. This does not mean that we will always get well of every disease. It does not mean that we can always bring back what randomness and brokenness rob from us. It does not mean that we can escape death, with the many different faces that death has. "Metanoia," or conversion of life, means turning over our whole being to God for his miracle of bringing life out of death.

Tragedy spells the end of many things at the earthly level; the tragic dimension cannot be removed from this present life. However, Jesus' cross and resurrection-triumph over tragedy provide the paradigm of hope that lies beyond all the deaths we are called upon to die. It is the promise of a different kind of "miracle" than is measurable in the physical world. Resurrection faith is a response to the mystery of evil and suffering, though it is not the satisfying rational "solution" that we may long for intellectually.

The title of a sermon I heard some years ago focuses well the Christian theology of suffering. The sermon was entitled "When There Is No Miracle." As long as things are going smoothly in life our faith is not really challenged. But when the storms come and our "Humpty Dumpty" worldview is shattered, the old self with its system of makeshift defenses falls under siege. It is no longer able to meet the level of stress and pain that we are now facing. In such times, our natural faith-instinct often is to ask for a miracle. "Oh God," we pray, "don't let this happen. Please do some great act of mercy to stop it. Use your power to prevent this awful thing or to change it."

But most of the time there is no "miracle" in the dictionary sense, because such miracles by definition are rare. Then faith is challenged to ask, "Why didn't God do something? Why didn't God step in? Where was God when we needed him?" The same compelling questions surround the death of Jesus, the execution of a wholly innocent man. No matter how many times we hear the story of the crucifixion, we are still moved to ask, where was God as the Roman soldiers were spitting upon the face of Jesus? Where was God as the thirty-nine lashes cut into his back? Where was God as the nails crushed the bones of his hands and feet? The words of the well-known Catholic theologian Hans Kung pound like a Roman hammer. Jesus, Kung says, died "a wordless, helpless, miracle-less, even God-less death."[55]

Some years ago the cartoon character Ziggy was depicted as standing desolate and alone atop a mountain, looking long-ingly heavenward. In the caption, Ziggy voices what many people feel in crisis: "Am I on hold?" This bit of humor actually conceals one of faith's most difficult challenges: Why doesn't God fix things so we do not have to suffer unjustly?

As I look back in my own life at those losses which I did not think I could bear, I often prayed for a miracle to happen. But there was no miracle. The forces of destruction moved relent-lessly on their way, quite heedless of my prayers. My child will always be severely disabled; my marriage ended forever.

Such times represent the hour of our own crucifixion, in which we find hope only by interpreting our lives through the Christ-paradigm. Walter Burghardt in his book *Sir, We Would Like to See Jesus* makes the link between Jesus' cross and ours:

> *You alone really know what nails crucify you. The question is, what do you do when "another fastens a belt around you and takes you where you do not wish to go" (Jn. 21:18)?*

*Does the folly of your cross make any sense to you? Have you
yet accepted the crucial Christian truth, that salvation comes
through crucifixion—yours as well as Christ's?*[56]

One of the great prayers of Christendom is in the Daily Office
of the Book of Common Prayer. It captures this same theme:

*Almighty God, whose most dear Son went not up to joy but
first he suffered pain, and entered not into glory before he
was crucified: Mercifully grant that we, walking in the way
of the cross, may find it none other than the way of life and
peace, through Jesus Christ your Son our Lord. Amen.*

The necessity of walking the Way of the Cross in our
healing journey is illuminated by the story of the Great
Confession. (Matthew 16:13-28) In this account Jesus inter-
rogates the disciples concerning his true identity. Simon
Peter, in his usual brash and uninhibited manner, boldly
declares that Jesus is indeed the long-awaited Messiah, the
Son of God. Jesus commends him for this statement, though
it is quickly apparent that Peter is far from a true understanding of what he has proclaimed.

Jesus can only provisionally accept the title Messiah,
because of the grievous misunderstanding of it in the popular thinking of the day. He begins to try to teach the disciples
the authentic role of the Messiah as one of suffering and ser-
vanthood, not political power and worldly success. He thus
places himself in the great tradition of Hebrew prophecy,
especially Second Isaiah and the vision of the "Suffering
Servant." Jesus tells the disciples that he is destined to suffer
and eventually die at the hands of the prevailing religious and
political establishment.

Simon Peter immediately begins to remonstrate with
Jesus: "God forbid, Lord! This shall never happen to you." His
reaction shows how deeply threatening Jesus' words were to
his followers, who at that time still understood his destiny as
one of earthly triumph. Jesus' response to Peter is quite

remarkable: "Get behind me, Satan! You are a hindrance to me; for you are not on the side of God, but of men." (Literally, "You are not thinking God's thoughts." 16:23) At no other time does Jesus ever refer to one of his disciples as satanic, except possibly Judas Iscariot at the hour of his betrayal.

In order to understand Jesus' extremely strong words to Peter, I believe that we must draw upon the story of Jesus' temptations in the desert as he began his public life. (Matthew 4:1-11 and Luke 4:1-13) There Jesus encounters Satan, who presents him with three temptations. (The Greek word means "trial," or "test.")

1. First, during the long days of fasting Jesus naturally becomes hungry. Satan urges him to abandon his fast and turn some of the desert stones into loaves of bread. This is the voice that says, "Avoid the pain of unfulfilled desires and hungers. Don't deprive yourself. Don't subject yourself to a life of self-discipline. Why should you? With your gifts, you can have what you want when you want it. The difficult way of self-denial can be avoided. You have the power to live above all that and escape from its demands. Turn these hard stones of self-sacrifice and self-giving into tasty bread whenever you please. You don't have to go by 'the steep way and the narrow door.' Let your appetites be your guide. Indulge them whenever you please."

But Jesus replied, "We don't find life just at the level of appetite; the higher way of communion with God must take precedence." (Literally: "Man does not live by bread alone, but by every word that proceeds from the mouth of God." Matthew 4:4)

2. In the second temptation Satan urges Jesus to jump off the pinnacle of the temple and demonstrate his unusual powers. This voice says, "Why challenge the prevailing culture? Why swim against the stream? Why confront the sickness and brokenness of society? This will only anger them. Instead, amuse them. Indulge them. Perform stunts that will entertain them. They will love you for it, and you will gain instant popularity. Make sure the press is there to see your performance

and time it so you will be on all the evening news shows. You will be a sensation, an overnight success. Why bother with all this 'integrity' business anyway? It will never sell. In fact, it will only get you into trouble with the authorities. Take the easy road and the short-cuts. Avoid the difficult path of suffering for what is right."

But Jesus said, "That would be an offense to God, whose way is holy and righteous." (Literally: "You shall not tempt the Lord your God." Matthew 4:7)

3. The third temptation encompasses the other two and is the epitome of all satanic enticements: "Fall down and worship me and you can have all the kingdoms of the world." This voice says, "Throw in your lot with all the exploitative forces of the world. Join the unscrupulous types who prey on the world's weak and defenseless. They may be religious charlatans, drug dealers, Wall Street inside traders, political opportunists, dishonest defense contractors, con artists, or whatever. But they're the ones who make it big, because they understand the ruling principle of this world: greed. They get it all. With your gifts you can rule any and all of these 'kingdoms.' That's where the real power is."

But Jesus replied: "Ultimate worth-ship lies only in God. Serving him ultimately brings the only true success in life." (Literally: "You shall worship the Lord your God and him only shall you serve." Matthew 4:10)

When Simon Peter began to "rebuke" Jesus, arguing strongly that he did not have to walk the way of vulnerability and self-sacrifice, Jesus knew that he was hearing once again that selfsame voice from the desert trials. The Evil One had promised that he would return at some opportune time. He had tried to divert Jesus at the beginning from a cruciform Messiahship; now he was back for one final momentous assault as the looming shadow of the Cross threatened the downfall of the demonic order. For that moment Peter was the mouthpiece of the universal message of Satan: We do not have to become our true self through suffering. We can find the easy route of avoidance and escape.

Only this background explains why Jesus reacted so strongly to Simon Peter that day. In some ways this "betrayal" was more subtle than the one soon to come through Judas. Peter's reflection of the sick and shallow expectations of popular culture invited Jesus to betray his true self, the mission for which he had come into the world. If Jesus had listened to Peter that day, the whole long drama of human salvation would have been aborted and would have had to begin all over.

When we listen to the destructive, "demonic" voices within us, we likewise risk the loss of ourselves and our unique destiny. These voices often say, "Your suffering is meaningless. Where is God in your pain? Why didn't he prevent it? Does he really care about you? You don't really have to go through the grief journey. You can take an easier way of addiction and escapism."

The story of Jesus' temptations is a paradigm to illuminate our own experience. We too have a "Messiahship" to carry out. We have been "anointed" to bring our unique gifts, our story, and our redemption-history into the service of humankind. To betray this mission is to succumb to the evil forces that are always inviting us to abandon our true self and abort the healing journey.

Jesus' story does not promise an easy out. It does not offer a magical solution. It is not like the Superman image, where the invincible one swoops down from the sky and saves the innocent at the right moment. The Resurrection miracle is of an entirely different kind than popular religion wants, different than our childish faith would ask. It is a miracle that comes only on the other side of a Cross. The miracle is God's power to give life back on the other side of pain, not the magical avoidance of pain.

H. A. Williams, the English theologian, has given one of the most profound contemporary reflections on the relationship of suffering and Resurrection. It is worth hearing at some length:

Suffering is experienced as a threat to what I am. It threatens to diminish and in the end to destroy my personal identity. It forces me to be less and less the person I once knew and

*felt myself to be until I cease to be that person at all.
Resurrection in this context means turning the threat into a
promise, so that what would otherwise destroy me becomes
the very means by which I am created…. Instead of ceasing
to live because of what I suffer, I live more fully and deeply
because of it….*

*We discover that the self we took as our total self was in
fact only a small fraction of what we are, that we have
reserves of strength, and insight and courage and heroism and
love and compassion of which so far we have been totally
unaware… So when the suffering first comes, ignorant of our
dormant potential, we feel simply that we cannot bear it….*

*Yet when, by miracle, we accept the suffering, receive it,
take it on board, then we find that this limited self is an illusion, that we are infinitely more than we ever imagined….
Thus does the destructive power of suffering become creative
and what is death-dealing become life-giving.*[57]

We cannot claim that this is a fully satisfactory "answer" to the
age-old problem of evil and suffering. The question of how
evil can exist in a world governed and created by a good God
will continue to haunt us.

Is it possible that a part of what it means to be human is
the acceptance for now of the mystery that surrounds this
issue? Could it be that a part of what is meant by the "Fall" of
Adam and Eve was their rebellion against the mystery of good
and evil? One of the tempter's chief lures was the promise that
"You will be as God, knowing good and evil." (Genesis 3:5) I
do not mean by this that we cannot raise questions about this
perennial thorn in the side of faith. I do not mean that we are
to deny our feelings of anger and outrage at the innocent suffering endured by ourselves and others. Finally, however, a
realistic faith does have to accept our inability to resolve the
problem of evil at the level of our present understanding.

Even the great saints and mystics ultimately have had to
bow before this unfathomable mystery. A prime example is
Julian of Norwich. During a period of critical illness Julian

received numerous "revelations" about the ways of God. She particularly asked for light on the problem of suffering. The emissary or mediator of her visions finally explained it was not possible to explain the problem in this present order of creation, but assured her that God would bring meaning out of it all. It was out of this experience that Julian's famous utterance was formed, so powerful in its simplicity: "All shall be well, and all shall be well, and all manner of thing shall be well."

The kind of "power" that God exerts against evil seems more paradoxical than we can fully comprehend. Theology has traditionally asserted the doctrine of God as "all-powerful," but in Dorothy Sayer's words God chose to "set it by" in order to invest the creation with order and freedom. The "something that power destroys" is, of course, this freedom. It is a pre-condition of our humanness, which evidently God supremely valued, even above a creation that presumably would have had to conform to God's will. As the late Bishop Stephen F. Bayne observed:

> *God put freedom into His created universe in order that the universe could respond to His love with an answering love of its own…. He put into the created universe a principle of choice; and He paid a two-fold price for that. First, He limited his own freedom to have everything His own way. Second, He committed Himself to having to win out of freedom what He could perfectly easily have commanded as a right.*[58]

Faith well knows that all pathways to Recovery must finally affirm hope full in the ugly face of evil and death. As Ira Nerken has said, "Recovery, after all, can be seen as life's bold act, affirming itself in angry defiance against death. The pain that leads to anger at the violation inflicted on one's meaning and purpose becomes the will to find a new meaning."[59]

In one of the most magnificent passages of the New Testament St. Paul asks, "Who will separate us from the love of Christ? Shall tribulation, or distress, or persecution, or famine, or nakedness, or peril or sword? No, in all these things we are more than conquerors through him who loved us." (Romans 8:35-37 NRSV) Notice most carefully what is said and what is not said here. St. Paul does not say that these things will never happen to us, or that by some miracle we who are God's people shall escape them. He says, rather, that *in* all these things we are more than conquerors. That is, we don't just win out, but we are given a higher order of life entirely—more than what we were before we suffered.

Some of the most comforting words in all of Scripture are found in the eighth chapter of Romans, although significant differences in meaning occur among the various translations. The New Revised Standard Version says: "We know that all things work together for good for those who love God, who are called according to his purpose." (Romans 8:28)

However, I believe that a much deeper insight is conveyed in the original Revised Standard translation: "We know that *in everything God works for good* with those who love him, who are called according to his purpose." The whole Biblical drama proclaims, not just that *things* work together for good, which is debatable, but that *God works in all things* to heal us and to redeem the human story and our individual stories.

This is the heart of Judeo-Christian faith. It is the trust that nothing, however tragic, is outside the power of God to transform. This is the real miracle of Recovery. It is the light of hope that shines in the midst of the long saga of human suffering and grief.

Chapter Six

The Art of
Consolation

Consolation is indeed an art. It is the art of active love… Wistful moments come when I recall what was, what is, and what might have been. As light displaces darkness, I recognize my debt to those who have been my comforters, and I pray that I have learned out of this experience both how to grieve and how to console.

—Troy Organ[60]

The Lord has given me the tongue of a teacher, that I may know how to sustain the weary with a word.

—Isaiah 50:4 (NRSV)

One of the surest signs that we are moving into grief Recovery is a growing awareness of others' pain and a willingness to help them in their grief journey. It is also one of the most powerful means of insuring our own continuing journey into wholeness. Twelve-step spirituality recognizes in the last step of the program how essential it is to our own spiritual health that we learn to share the healing resources that we have discovered:

Having had a spiritual awakening as the result of these Steps, we tried to carry this message to [other grieving people], and to practice these principles in all our affairs.

This becomes especially important in view of the general lack of support for grieving people in our culture. We are often less understanding of grief than of many other kinds of personal struggles. As Bernadine Kreis and Alice Pattie have observed:

> *If you are an alcoholic, juvenile delinquent, an unmarried mother, an abandoned baby, or just getting old, society is there to cushion your problem. You can get help. But if you are in grief you soon discover that not only are you on your own in your trouble, but that few people really know how to help you.*[61]

There is an urgent need in our society for better skills in helping people through the grief process. It hardly needs saying that the best "school" for learning such skills is going through a grief journey yourself. As with other profound human experiences, ultimately only those who have grieved can fully understand grief. Therefore, those who have made the journey are in the best position to offer the most help to other grieving persons.

Following some basic guidelines in grief work will enable us to be more effective. This chapter sets forth six tested principles. These guidelines will allay some of the anxieties that you may initially experience by affirming that the ability to listen is far more therapeutic than our usual anxious efforts at explaining, reassuring, and giving "right" answers.

It is especially important for non-professionals—neighbors, friends, and relatives—to become skillful and comfortable in helping grieving people, because so much of the work must be done by them. It is impossible for the various helping professionals to be at all the places where people are grieving, and the lay helper often has a special kind of access that is not open to the professional.

1. The first and most important rule in grief ministry is to listen to the grieving person, and then to listen some more! Listening enables us to determine which of the periods of grief the person is in. It is impossible to be helpful if we treat per-

sons still in Reaction, for example, as if they were ready to move into Recovery. As Kreis and Pattie have aptly noted, it is too often true that "in shock [Reaction] you are expected to share your grief, as if it were real grief, which it is not; when you are suffering [in Realization], you are expected to be recovering, which you are not."[62] The main reason for insisting on the priority of listening, however, is simply that it is so therapeutic. The person who is truly listened-to senses that she is being treated with respect, compassion, and love. These are the most powerfully healing gifts that we have to give each other.

Dr. Wayne Oates, my former teacher, liked to say, "The Lord gave us two ears and only one mouth. That should tell us something." Indeed, it ought to tell us that what we say to grieving persons has far less power than how we listen to them. One of the most common fears in reaching out to the grieving is that "I won't know what to say." This anxiety can be greatly relieved by the understanding that persons in grief will be helped far more by our ears than by our tongues.

There are a couple of obvious but important corollaries of the listening principle. One is to avoid questioning a grieving person. Somehow we find it natural to fall into this mistake. For example, it is good to avoid the usual "What did the doctor say?" "What do they think happened?" "Don't you think you ought to...?" Open-ended statements are likely to be more helpful: "I've been thinking of you a lot since this happened." "I wanted to come by and see you today." "I know this has been a very difficult time for you." Such statements invite grieving people to tell us where they are, what their real feelings are, and what they need to "register" with another person. Questions, on the other hand, restrict people and compel them to follow the questioner's agenda instead of the inner one that they may need to express.

Another corollary of listening is to avoid talking about oneself. An easy trap is to talk about "When my mother died..." or "Now, when my sister went through this..." These comments generally violate the listening principle and force grieving persons to expend energy attending to information which cannot currently benefit them.

2. A second important principle in dealing with grieving persons is to avoid reassuring. This often runs squarely against our grain, because nothing seems more natural than to say things like "You're going to get over this in time." "Don't you think it was better for him to go this way?" (Only the grieving person is entitled to decide that.) An especially hurtful one is, "But just look at all that you still have to be thankful for." This says to the grieving person, "You are not really entitled to grieve. Your hurt is no worse than that of many others. You are just feeling sorry for yourself. You should stifle these feelings." This may not be intended, but it is almost certainly what is conveyed.

Feeling the need to reassure provides a ready-made invitation to trot out all the old standard cliches: "It's all for the best." "There's a reason for everything." "We have to be strong." "Time heals all wounds" (ignoring the fact, as someone has wisely observed, that time also wounds all heals). "Don't you think good will come of it?" Or that all-time heresy: "It was God's will."

The trouble with reassuring is that it conveys, how ever subtly, a very unhelpful message. It says "How you feel isn't as important as how I *want* you to feel." Unconsciously we may be wanting the grieving person to feel better, so that we won't have to continue to feel his suffering ourselves. This is quite the opposite of being willing to meet people where they are and really listen to them. While we do not mean it to be so, attempts to reassure tend to block the grieving person's chance to share feelings, thus obstructing one of the human spirit's most vital channels to recovery.

3. A third and closely related guideline is to avoid giving answers and advice. Especially in the earlier phases of grief, people usually are not seeking factual information or objective answers to theological questions. Creative listening often will discern that the question is in fact an indirect way of expressing their deep pain over the loss, rather than a request for theological discussion. Instead of our immediately getting hooked

by the surface-level of a question like, "Why did this happen?", it may be more helpful to say something open-ended like, "I can see how painful it is for you that this happened." This offers people an invitation to share the feelings that may be lurking beneath the question.

In the section on Realization in Chapter One, we noted that grieving persons often raise such difficult questions as "Do you think God causes such things?" or "Why did God let this happen?" In the early period of grief, however, these questions may actually be a way of saying, "I am feeling desperate... confused... frightened... depressed..." or a host of grief's other emotions. Listening actively and creatively for the feelings underneath keeps us from getting sidetracked onto "head-level" discussions, which the person may not be able to benefit from until later in the grief process.

4. A fourth rule is that tears are okay. The saints used to speak of "the gift of tears." Indeed, tears are one of God's sublime gifts in behalf of emotional healing. They are usually a sign that we have been touched by an awareness of being loved, understood, and listened to. Our protective defenses are thereby relaxed, and we are able to get in touch with feelings that really matter and need to be incorporated into consciousness.[63]

The inexperienced are sometimes distressed or even panicked when someone breaks into tears. They think they have worsened the person's condition and caused him to sink into deeper pain. Probably the opposite is true. Weeping is momentarily painful of course, but it is generally a sign that feelings have been touched and thereby a healthy step toward recovery is being taken. Robert Veninga has eloquently described the relationship between tears and the full embracing of the Realization of our loss:

> *...you need to enter fully into your tragedy. You need to feel in the depth of your being what it is that you have lost. You should talk about your losses over and over again with a sympathetic friend. And you need to let the tears flow when your world is spinning out of control. In short, you need to*

acknowledge the enormity of that which has happened.[64]

The "gift of tears" will come harder for most men in our society because of the macho image purveyed by media advertising, "hero" movies, and the "Marlboro Man." Males are often taught that true masculinity means never crying (or expressing any emotion), since he-men must always be "cool." This particular piece of cultural folly takes a heavy toll among males in the form of increased hypertension, cardiac problems, and gastro-intestinal disorders, as well as rendering the grief process more difficult.

5. A fifth important rule is to let grieving persons talk about their loss. A natural mistake is to assume that if they start reminiscing, they will regress into greater sadness or upset. Again, the reverse is far more likely to happen. One of the key ways that we work through grief is to replay memories of the meaningful experiences associated with the object of loss. Sometimes this may try the patience of the ministering person, but it is an essential part of the recovery process. As one grieving mother said about those seeking to be helpful, "Ignoring the deceased is the worst thing someone can do."

A corollary of this is that it is important to avoid euphemisms and indirectness with the bereaved. Making references like "the problem" or "the situation" or "after what happened," instead of speaking directly, can convey subtly that we think it is all too terrible to face. The grieving person will likely pick up this cue, even unconsciously, and find it a damper on the expression of genuine feelings. It is more encouraging to say things like, "It sounds as though you and your Dad really enjoyed sailing." "You two must have had a great vacation that year." "I can see that moving meant leaving behind a lot of good friends." "So before you got sick, you were quite a golfer."

Particularly as the stage of Realization moves toward Recovery, people often feel a strong need to reminisce about happy times. This is an indispensable part of reformulating a future without that which has been lost. Jacqueline L. Rogers in her book, *I Want to Help But I Don't Know How*, speaks poignantly of this:

> *I hear you stumbling for words. Relax. There are no words…. On days when I can laugh, I will. On days when I can speak of my loved one, I need you to share my memories…. You don't have to give me answers, for I will learn to live without them. You don't have to pretend my loved one never existed, thinking I will forget if you do. Let me speak his name, and you speak it, too. He is always there, that one I love so deeply, always part of who I am. If you take that from me, I will be less than who I am.*[65]

6. The sixth and final rule is to relax and let your caring show. Ultimately, the most helpful thing that we have to offer grieving persons is just our caring presence. Genuine concern will come across, even if we are not always expert in what we say and do. It is all too easy to fall into a pattern of avoiding people in grief, because our anxiety over doing the wrong thing gets control of us. But not making contact at all will likely be more hurtful than merely saying something inept. Love can shine through ineptitude, but hardly through absence.

Perhaps it cannot be overstated that the heart of all grief ministry is meeting people where they are and offering the simple gifts of caring and "loving listening." In the early years of my ministry as a priest, Margaret, a parishioner who had also been a dear family friend for many years, was stricken with cancer. She was in her mid-forties with a devoted husband and three children. After a mastectomy, she struggled against her illness valiantly, but in those years treatment was not nearly so effective as now. During that period I was deeply impressed by Dr. Elizabeth Kubler-Ross's classic work, *On Death and Dying*, and had probably read her five-stage outline of the grief process in far too wooden a fashion. She presents the stages as (1) Denial and Isolation, (2) Anger, (3) Bargaining, (4) Depression, and (5) Acceptance.[66] (See the cautions in Chapter One about the concept of "stages" of grief.)

In any case, it became my conviction that my task as Margaret's pastor was to lead her to the final stage of "acceptance." During visits I tried to bring the best resources of pastoral care that I knew how to do. But Margaret did not move toward acceptance. As her condition worsened and she was forced beyond denial, she alternated mostly between anger and depression. She was not one bit ready to die. She dearly loved life and wanted to stay right here on earth and finish raising her children.

My attempts at ministry were complicated by the fact that I knew inside that I would have felt exactly the same in her situation, and probably would not have been half so brave. I was deeply frustrated by my sense of failure as a pastor, and wondered on each visit what I could do or say that would be even remotely helpful? Finally one day in near despair I called an older and far more experienced priest, who had spent many years as a chaplain in a large metropolitan hospital. I explained how painful it was that I could not seem to help Margaret reach the "acceptance stage" in her grief journey.

He said to me, "That is not your job. Margaret may not be able to reach acceptance. Allow her to be wherever she is. Your task is just to be with her and make sure you are there for her." The advice seemed simple and obvious afterward, but I doubt if I could have reached this insight alone. I did my best to follow this wise course to the day that Margaret died.

This story reminds us once again that all our attempts, finally, to analyze grief into "stages" will suffer from being artificial. They are only conceptual forms to help us sketch an imperfect map of the very complex terrain of human emotions. They can seem quite cold and contrived when placed alongside a grieving person. Therefore, we dare not in some Procrustean fashion force the individual journeys of people into too-rigid conceptual models. Heeding the guidelines outlined here will help to reduce our natural anxiety and increase our confidence in working with grieving people. Often we will have the rewarding sense of being agents of new life for some of our fellow pilgrims "who, in this transitory life, are in trouble, sorrow, need, sickness, or any other adversity."[67]

As grieving persons, we will certainly need to monitor our own journeys to determine when we are ready to work with others in grief. In the early period, we may feel that we will never again be able to listen to another's grief story. A part of Recovery, however, is that this feeling changes, and we find that we have something to offer other struggling people that we could have gained only from making the journey ourselves. As Ira Nerken says: "A tenet of all major faiths is that suffering can redeem, and that if we take its lessons to heart, we will better understand not only the meaning of our own lives and the precious gift that is life, but how to bring the gift of meaning, life and love to others who suffer."[68]

There is a story about a little girl who was late getting home from school one day. When she finally arrived, her mother inquired as to what had happened. The little girl said, "Well, Mommy, I was walking home with my friend Susie, and she dropped her doll and broke it." "Oh, I see," said the mother. "So you stayed to help her fix it." "No, Mommy," said the little girl, "I stayed to help her cry." That is the essence of the art of consolation.

Conclusion

Beyond Grief

All which I took from thee I did but take,
Not for thy harms,
But just that thou might'st seek it in My arms.
All which thy child's mistake
Fancies as lost, I have stored for thee at home:
　　Rise, clasp My hand, and come.

　　—Francis Thompson[69]

The troubles and sorrows, caused by our perversity, the Lord Jesus
takes, and lifts up to heaven where they are transformed to things of
delight and pleasure greater than heart can think or tongue can tell.
And when we get there ourselves we shall find them waiting for us
changed into things of beautiful and eternal worth.

　　—Julian of Norwich[70]

Weeping may spend the night, but joy comes in the morning.

　　—Psalm 30:6

It is the goal of the healing journey to reach that place of new
life in which we can finally let go of our loss and accept the
gift of recovery. We undergo the long hours, days, and years

of suffering in order to reach that "promised land" where our souls find a new home. One of the best descriptions of what it means to recover from grief has been given by Robert Bellah:

> *The deepest truth I have discovered is that if one accepts the loss, if one gives up clinging to what is irretrievably gone, then the nothing which is left is not barren but enormously fruitful. Everything that one has lost comes flooding back again out of the darkness, and one's relation to it is new— free and unclinging. But the richness of the nothing contains far more, it is the all-possible, it is the spring of freedom.*[71]

How do we get to this place of freedom and joy? The answer is that we can reach it only by making the healing journey. It is a stringent and arduous way, and often will seem to demand of us more strength than we have. To be "saved by our faith," an expression that Jesus often used, means to trust the promise that we shall be sustained by that Healing Power that is greater than our pain, and that the journey is worth it.

At the end of one of "The Chronicles of Narnia," C. S. Lewis has said all of this in a most imaginative and compelling way. On one of their voyages to the mystic land of Narnia, the children are given a glimpse of "Heaven," and of course they want to remain there in the companionship of the great Lion, Aslan, a symbol for Christ. However, they discover that they can only reach this glorious country from their own world. They meet a beautiful Lamb, who converses with them:

> "Please, Lamb," said Lucy, "is this the way to Aslan's country?"
>
> "Not for you," said the Lamb. "For you the door into Aslan's country is from your own world."
>
> "What!" said Edmund. "Is there a way into Aslan's country from our world too?"
>
> "There is a way into my country from all the worlds," said the Lamb, but as he spoke his snowy white flushed into tawny gold and his size changed and

he was Aslan himself, towering above them and scattering light from his mane.

"Oh, Aslan," said Lucy. "Will you tell us how to get into your country from our world?"

"I shall be telling you all the time," said Aslan. "But I will not tell you how long or short the way will be; only that it lies across a river. But do not fear that, for I am the great Bridge Builder."[72]

Our grief journeys do indeed have to be made from "our own world." We cannot enter anyone else's world, and no one else can grieve for us. We begin all such pilgrimages by accepting ourselves just where we are. We must also refuse every temptation to compare our journey with anyone else's. We cannot follow their pace, or imitate their way of grieving. Aslan does not tell us how long or short the way will be, only that it will be across a river. The river of grief will often seem deep and wide, but we have the promise of One who will be with us always to help us build bridges across the rivers of our pain.

As long as we live this side of Aslan's country, we shall continue to be wounded by the circumstances of a finite and broken world, and we shall grieve. But resources for recovery are available, whereby we discover with the ancient psalmist God's power to "restore the soul" (Psalm 23). Our ultimate healing, however, lies beyond this present world in the new order that God is preparing. Nowhere is this promise more beautifully expressed than in the Book of the Revelation:

> Then I saw a new heaven and a new earth; for the first heaven and the first earth had passed away, and the sea was no more.... And I heard a loud voice from the throne saying, "See, the home of God is among mortals.... He will wipe away every tear from their eyes. Death will be no more; mourning and crying and pain will be no more, for the first things have passed away." (NRSV 21:1, 3-4)

Thus, grieving will be brought to an end forever, and our long pilgrimage will reach its fulfillment beyond the realm of all that has power to break the human heart.

Continuing the Journey

The literature on grief and personal growth is vast indeed. This highly selective list contains only those resources that have been the most helpful in the author's own journey.

Beattie, Melody, *Codependent No More*. Center City, MN, Hazelden Foundation, 1987. A basic manual for identifying and overcoming the patterns of codependency. Several useful checklists.

Bradshaw, John, *Bradshaw on the Family*. Health Communications, Inc., Deerfield Beach, FL, 1988. Great insights into family systems and personal growth. Bradshaw is most gifted in integrating theological and psychological wisdom.

Burnett, Frances Hodgson, *The Secret Garden*, New York, Harper and Row, 1962. c. 1911. A classic parable of recovery from grief. Told as a children's story, but will delight and nurture adult children as well.

Claypool, John, *Tracks of a Fellow Struggler*. Waco, TX, Word Books, 1974. An honest and eloquent account by a clergyman who lost his nine-year-old daughter to leukemia.

Clinebell, Howard, *Growing Through Grief*. EcuFilm, 810 Twelfth Ave., Nashville, TN 37203. A videotape series of six sessions, with excellent practical resources for starting a grief group.

Despelder, Lynn Ann and Albert Lee Strickland, *The Last Dance: Encountering Death and Dying*, Mountain View, CA, Mayfield Publishing Co., 1991. A widely used and highly respected textbook of encyclopedic proportions for grief workers and specialists.

Fisher, Bruce, *Rebuilding: When Your Relationship Ends.* San Luis Obispo, CA, Impact Publishers, 1981. A compassionate and insightful outline of the path to recovery from divorce by an experienced divorce counselor.

Fowler, James, *Stages of Faith: The Psychology of Human Development and the Quest for Meaning.* New York, Harper and Row, 1981. A seminal work on faith development, creatively applying the pioneering efforts of Piaget, Kohlberg, and Erickson to the field of spiritual growth.

Halpern, Howard M., *How to Break Your Addiction to a Person.* New York, McGraw-Hill, 1982. A "bible" for those seeking help with relationship-addiction, but full of insight about early personality formation for anyone.

Hammarskjöld, Dag, *Markings.* New York, Alfred A. Knopf, 1964. Foreword by W. H. Auden. The spiritual journal of the second Secretary-General of the United Nations.

"How to Comfort Those Who Mourn." A useful pamphlet capsuling grief ministry, available from Kairos, Box 24306, Minneapolis, MN 55424.

Jones, Alan W., *Soul Making: The Way of Desert Spirituality.* Harper San Francisco, 1989 paperback edition. A compelling meditation on the theme of "dying in order to live."

Julian of Norwich, *Revelations of Divine Love*, translated by Clifton Wolters. New York and London, Penguin Books, 1966.

Kreis, Bernadine, and Alice Pattie, *Up From Grief: Patterns of Recovery.* Seabury Press, 1969. Now published by Phoenix Press, New York, 1984. An older but still valuable presentation of the grief process, with many practical helps.

Kubler-Ross, Elizabeth, *On Death and Dying*. New York, Macmillan, 1969. A classic by a pioneer in the field, presenting the grief process in five stages.

Kushner, Harold S., *When Bad Things Happen to Good People*. New York, Schocken Books, 1981. A rabbi's best-seller on the problem of evil. Fine wisdom on grieving in Chapter 6.

Lewis, C. S., *A Grief Observed*. London, Faber and Faber, 1961. A chronicle of the great Christian apologist's bout with despair and doubt after the death of his beloved wife.

Lindemann, Eric, "Symptomatology and Management of Acute Grief," *American Journal of Psychiatry*, 101, (1944), pp. 141-148. A ground-breaking article which helped to initiate our modern understanding of the grief process.

Marty, Martin E., *A Cry of Absence: Reflections for the Winter of the Heart*. Hagerstown, MD, Harper Torchbooks, 1986. Offers gracious and sensitive permission for both "wintery" and "summery" personalities to cherish their respective identities.

May, Gerald G., *Addiction and Grace*. San Francisco, Harper and Row, 1988. An important contribution to the growing awareness that addiction has many faces and is a universal malady, with creative integration of psychology and spirituality.

Nerken, Ira, "Making It Safe to Grieve," *Christian Century*, November 30, 1988, 1091-1094. A moving article written after the author's wife was killed by a hit-and-run driver. Shows that our culture is not always a safe place to grieve.

Oates, Wayne, *Pastoral Care and Counseling in Grief and Separation*. Philadelphia, Fortress Press, 1976. Practical help for those seeking to grow in "the art of consolation" by one of the fathers of modern pastoral theology.

Organ, Troy, "Grief and the Art of Consolation," *Christian Century*, August 1-8, 1979, 759-762. The author's wisdom about helping others, gained from mourning the death of his wife.

Peck, M. Scott, *The Road Less Traveled*. New York, Simon and Schuster, 1978. Deserves all of the adulation it has received for its profound insight into emotional and spiritual growth.

Raines, John C., "The Goodness of Grief," *Christian Century*, October 15, 1986, 886-887. The title captures the theme of this sensitive article.

Sanford, John, editor, *Fritz Kunkel: Selected Writings*. New York, Paulist Press, 1984. Renders a fine service to modern psychology of religion by reprinting the major works of a great Jungian. Sanford's own introductions and comments enrich the book.

Smedes, Lewis B., *Forgive and Forget: Healing the Hurts We Don't Deserve*. San Francisco, Harper and Row, 1984. An excellent testimony to the complexity of forgiveness and the importance of understanding it as a process.

Stearns, Ann Kaiser, *Living through Personal Crisis*. New York, Ballantine Books, 1984. A popular and practical work on growth through grief, covering a wide variety of issues.

Westberg, Granger, *Good Grief*. Philadelphia, Fortress Press, 1962. Excellent delineation of the grief experience by a noted pastoral counselor.

Wiederkehr, Macrina, *A Tree Full of Angels*, San Francisco, Harper and Row, 1988. A celebration of finding God in

ordinary life, reminiscent of Brother Lawrence, by a gifted poet and spiritual director. Even the prose in this beautiful book is "poetry."

Williams, H. A., *True Resurrection*. New York, Harper Colophon
Books, 1972. A brilliant translation of the meaning of the
Resurrection into the language of recovery and spiritual
growth.

Notes

1.   Stanley Jasspon Kunitz, (1905-) *Anthology of Magazine Verse and Yearbook of American Poetry*, 1980 Edition. Edited by Alan F. Pater. Monitor Book Company, Inc., Beverly Hills, CA, 1980, pp. 227-228.

2.   Anne Tyler, *The Accidental Tourist*, 1988. From the movie soundtrack.

3.   Quoted in "Dealing With Grief," The Christophers, 12 East 48th St., New York, N. Y. 10017.

4.   *Collected Works*, Vol. 17, p. 200.

5.   Quoted in "Finding God in Pain or Illness," by Susan Saint Sing, Abbey Press, St. Meinrad, IN, 1988, p. 5.

6.   T. S. Eliot, *The Four Quartets*, Now York, Harcourt, Brace, Jovanovich, 1943, 1971, Section 111, p. 29.

7.   "The Goodness of Grief," *Christian Century*, October 15, 1986, p. 886.

8.   Lynne Ann Despelder and Albert Lee Strickland, *The Last Dance: Encountering Death and Dying*, p. 261.

9.   *Op. cit.*, pp. 258-259.

10.   All names have been changed.

11.   Quoted in "Losing Someone Close," by Robert DiGiulio, Abbey Press, St. Meinrad, IN, 1988, p. 5.

12. Alan Jones, *Soul Making: The Way of Desert Spirituality*, Harper San Francisco, 1989, p. 71.

13. David Steindl-Rast, *A Listening Heart, The Art of Contemplative Living*, New York, Crossroads, 1983, p. 12.

14. Dag Hammarskjöld, *Markings*, New York, Alfred A. Knopf, 1964, p. 205.

15. John Bradshaw, "Our Families, Ourselves," *Lear's* magazine, April, 1989, p. 55.

16. John C. Raines, "The Goodness of Grief," *Christian Century*, October 15, 1986, p. 887.

17. *Markings*, page 197.

18. Lewis B. Smedes, *Forgive and Forget: Healing the Hurts We Don't Deserve*, pp. 1-37. Despite the title, Dr. Smedes makes it very clear that forgiving is not the same as forgetting. (pp. 38 ff.)

19. From the Associated Press, July 20, 1996. The book is entitled *Bound to Forgive—the Pilgrimage to Reconciliation of a Beirut Hostage*.

20. *Bradshaw on the Family*, Health Communications Publications, 1988, *passim*.

21. One of the finest contemporary analyses of the meaning of love is found in M. Scott Peck's renowned work, *The Road Less Traveled*. A most helpful aspect of Dr. Peck's discussion is in his delineation of the pitfalls in the common experience of "falling in love," which of course, is the major focus of love as a feeling in our culture. See Chapter II, pp. 81-182. Perhaps our English language could serve us better if we learned to employ the word "like" to express love as a feeling, and reserved "love" only for love's attitudinal expression. We do

not really choose to *like* someone, anymore than we choose favorite foods, colors, and aesthetic tastes. This demonstrates that liking is a feeling, and should not be confused with the attitude of love. This confusion is seen when we say "I love chocolate, raspberries, the color red," or claim to be, "in love" with someone we hardly know. Clearly the word "like" describes far better what is meant. Liking and disliking refer to the experience of pleasure. Loving has to do with moral and spiritual choice.

22. *The Interpreter's Bible*, Nashville, Abingdon, Volume 7, p. 314.

23. "Homily Service," The Liturgical Conference, June, 1989, p. 31.

24. Rokelle Lerner, editor, *Daily Affirmations*, Pompano Beach, FL, Health Communications, for June 21, pp. 172 and 190.

25. Arthur Miller, *After the Fall*, New York, Viking Press, 1964, Act I, p. 24.

26. "Embracing Your Memories: A Journey of Healing for Lent," Creative Communications, St. Louis, 1988, p. 29.

27. Quoted in "Forward Day by Day," Forward Movement Publications, Cincinnati, May-July, 1989, p. 94.

28. James W. Fowler, *Stages of Faith*, *passim*. See a chart of the seven stages, p. 113.

29. Op. cit., p. 149.

30. Ibid.

31. Op. cit., p. 150.

32. See *Fritz Kunkel: Selected Writings*, New York, Paulist, pp. 140-154 and *passim*.

33. Op. cit., p. 228.

34. St. Mary's Press, Winona, Minnesota, 1990, p. 132.

35. Op. cit., p. 186.

36. Edna St.Vincent Millay, in *Days of Healing, Days of Joy*, by Ernie Larson and Carol Larson Hagerty, Hazelden Foundation, 1987, meditation for July 6.

37. See the excellent analysis of "Dependency," in M. Scott Peck's book, *The Road Less Traveled*, New York, Touchstone Books, 1978, pp. 98-105.

38. Hazelden Foundation, 1987, quoted on front panel. Instead of saying "in ourselves" I would prefer to say "in our God-Self."

39. Gerald G. May, *Addiction and Grace*, San Francisco, Harper and Row, 1988, pp. 94-95. See also the section on "Idealization," in Chapter 9 of Ann Kaiser Stearns' book, *Living through Personal Crisis*.

40. Op. cit., pp. 94-95.

41. Op. cit., p. 96.

42. Fritz Kunkel, *Creation Continues*, Mahwah, NJ, Paulist, Press, 1987, p. 140. (First published, 1946)

43. Op. cit., pp. 97-98.

44. Bug and Bear Music and Home Sweet Home Music, from the album "Never Alone," Amy Grant, © 1980. Word Incorporated, Waco, TX.

45. "On Prayer," Forward Movement Publications, Cincinnati, OH, p. 3. Reprinted from *When I Became a Man*, New York, Oxford Press.

46. *Markings*, p. 97.

47. *Markings*, W. H. Auden's Foreword, pp. xv-xvi.

48. Quoted in "Finding God in Pain or Illness," by Susan Saint Sing, Abbey Press, St. Meinrad, IN, 1988, p. 3.

49. Abraham J. Heschel, *A Passion for Truth*, New York, Farrar, Straus, & Giroux, 1973, p. 301.

50. Episcopal Book of Common Prayer, p. 394.

51. John Sanford, editor, *Fritz Kunkel: Selected Writings*, pp. 207-208.

52. From "The Devil to Pay," Masterpieces of Religious Verse, New York, Harper and Row, #592, p. 189.

53. Kalil Gibran, "On Pain," *The Prophet*, New York, Alfred A. Knopf, 1923, 195 1, pp. 58-59.

54. See Bernhard W. Anderson, *Understanding the Old Testament*, Prentice-Hall, Third Edition, p. 111.

55. See *Synthesis*, St. Luke's School of Theology, Sewanee, TN, March 19, 1989, p. 4.

56. Walter Burghardt, *Sir, We Would See Jesus*, New York, Paulist Press, 1982, pp. 63-64.

57. H. A. Williams, *True Resurrection*, New York, Harper Colophon Books, 1972, pp. 144, 153-154.

58. Quoted in *Forward Day by Day*, for September 14, 1994, p. 47. Forward Movement Publications, Cincinnati, Ohio, 1994.

59. Ira Nerken, "Making It Safe to Grieve," *Christian Century*, November 30, 1988, pp. 1093-1094.

60. Troy Organ, "Grief and the Art of Consolation," *Christian Century*, August 1-8, 1979, p. 762.

61. Kreis and Pattie, *Up from Grief*, Seabury, p. 9.

62. Op. cit., p. 36.

63. See "Tears That Speak," by Gregg Levoy, *Psychology Today*, July-August, 1988, pp. 8-9. Research by William Frey of Minneapolis suggests that tears may actually remove certain stress-causing chemicals from the body.

64. Robert Veninga, *A Gift of Hope*, Little, Brown, 1985, p. 66.

65. Quoted in "Losing Someone Close," by Robert DiGiulio, Abbey Press, St. Meinrad, IN, 1988, p. 3.

66. Elizabeth Kubler-Ross, *On Death and Dying*, New York, Macmillan, 1969. See her outline of the stages on p. 264.

67. The Episcopal Book of Common Prayer, p. 329.

68. "Making It Safe to Grieve," *Christian Century*, November 30, 1988, p. 1094.

69. Francis Thompson, *The Hound of Heaven*, Harrisburg, PA, Morehouse Publishing, p. 26.

70. Julian of Norwich, *Revelations of Divine Love*, New York/London, Penguin Books, 1966, p. 139.

71. Robert N. Bellah, *Beyond Belief*, New York, Harper and Row, 1970, pp. xx-xxi.

72. C. S. Lewis, *The Voyage of the Dawn Treader*, New York, Collier, p. 215.

Other Books of Related Interest from Morehouse Publishing Group and Trinity Press International

Spiritual Care of Dying and Bereaved People
by Penelope Wilcock

Offers detailed examples of how to relate to a terminally ill person in a meaningful way and become "a gentle companion on the journey toward death." Shows how to be a source of comfort, how to listen quietly, and how to create a positive context for the dying person to approach the end of life. Includes advice on resolving unfinished business—including reconciling with and forgiving others, handling financial concerns, and dealing with ongöing medical needs.

God Is No Illusion
Meditations on the End of Life
by John Tully Carmody

Powerful, deeply moving psalms on the end of life that deal with serious illness, aging, and death. Included are 15 letters on the process of the author's struggle with bone cancer.

"With his typical humor, self-effacement and insight, John Carmody has produced a contemporary psalter of laments and praise songs that is sure to lead many people through the valley of the shadow of pain and suffering."
—Publishers Weekly

Making Sense Out of Sorrow
A Journey of Faith
by The Rev. Foster R. McCurley and Rabbi Alan G. Weitzman

The ideal book for those who are looking for a source of comfort while grieving the loss of a loved one. Written from a Judeo-Christian perspective, this small book provides hope from one's religious traditions.

"...powerful and penetrating insights that will bring to all grieving hearts understanding and solace." —Rabbi Dr. Earl A. Grollman, author of *Living When A Loved One Has Died*